The Believer's Secret of Living Like Christ

D0012978

The Believer's Secret of Living Like Christ

ANDREW MURRAY

BETHANY HOUSE PUBLISHERS
MINNEAPOLIS, MINNESOTA 55438
A Division of Bethany Fellowship, Inc.

Copyright © 1985
Bethany House Publishers
All Rights Reserved

Published by Bethany House Publishers
A Division of Bethany Fellowship, Inc.
6820 Auto Club Road, Minneapolis, Minnesota 55438

Printed in the United States of America

Library of Congress Cataloging in Publication Data

Murray, Andrew, 1828-1917.
   The believer's secret of living like Christ.

   (Andrew Murray Christian maturity library)
   1. Christian life. I. Title. II. Series.
BV4501.M79713   1985   248.4   85-26683
ISBN 0-87123-445-9

ANDREW MURRAY was born in South Africa in 1828. After receiving his education in Scotland and Holland, he returned to that land and spent many years there as both pastor and missionary. He was a staunch advocate of biblical Christianity. He is best known for his many devotional books.

Books by Andrew Murray

ANDREW MURRAY CHRISTIAN MATURITY LIBRARY

The Believer's Absolute Surrender
The Believer's Call to Commitment
The Believer's Full Blessing of Pentecost
The Believer's New Covenant
The Believer's New Life
The Believer's Prophet, Priest and King
The Believer's Secret of a Perfect Heart
The Believer's Secret of Holiness
The Believer's Secret of Living Like Christ
The Believer's Secret of Obedience
The Believer's Secret of Spiritual Power
The Believer's Secret of the Master's Indwelling
The Spirit of Christ

ANDREW MURRAY PRAYER LIBRARY

The Believer's Prayer Life
The Believer's School of Prayer
The Ministry of Intercessory Prayer
The Secret of Believing Prayer

ANDREW MURRAY DEVOTIONAL LIBRARY

The Believer's Daily Renewal
The Believer's Secret of Intercession
The Believer's Secret of the Abiding Presence
The Believer's Secret of Waiting on God
Day by Day with Andrew Murray

How to Raise Your Children for Christ

Contents

Introduction

In writing this book on the image of our blessed Lord, and the likeness to Him to which we are called, I have two remarks by way of preface.

The first is that no one is more conscious than I of the difficulty of the task I have undertaken, and ultimately of its human limitations. There were two things I tried to do: (1) *To draw a portrait of the Son of God*, "in all things made like unto his brethren," showing how, in the reality of His human life, we have an exact pattern of what the Father wants us to be. This portrait should make likeness to Him infinitely and mightily attractive, should arouse desire, awaken love, inspire hope, and strengthen faith in all who are seeking to imitate Jesus Christ. (2) *To draw a portrait of the believer* as he, with some degree of spiritual exactness, really reflects this image, and amid the trials and duties of daily life proves that likeness to Christ is no mere ideal, but through the power of the Holy Spirit is a most blessed reality.

How often and how deeply I have felt, after having sought to describe a particular characteristic of the believer's life, how utterly insufficient human thoughts are to grasp, or human words to express, that spiritual beauty of which one at best only has seen faint glimpses! And how often our very thoughts deceive us, as they give us some human conception of what the Word reveals, while we lack that true vision of the spiritual glory of Him who is the brightness of the Father's glory!

The second remark I wish to make is a suggestion as to what I think is needed for the believer to behold the glory of the image into which we are to be changed. I was impressed some time ago with the practice a kindergarten class had on object lessons. A picture was shown them, which they were told to look at carefully. They then had to shut their eyes and take time to think and remember everything they had seen. Next, the picture was removed, and the little ones had to tell all they could remember seeing. Again the picture was shown, and they were to try to notice what they had not observed before; again to shut their eyes and think, and again to tell what more they had noticed. And then once more, until every line of the picture had been taken in. As I looked at the keen interest with which the little eyes gazed on the picture, and then were pressed so tightly shut as they tried to realize, and take in, and keep what they had been looking at, I felt that if our Bible reading were more of such an object lesson, the unseen spiritual realities pictured to us in the Word would take much deeper hold of our inner life. We are too easily content with the thoughts suggested by the words of the Bible, though these are but forms of truth, without giving time for the substantial spiritual reality to get lodged and rooted in the heart.

Let us, in meditating on the image of God in Christ, to which we are to be conformed, remember this. When some special trait has occupied our thoughts, let us shut our eyes, and open our hearts; let us think, and pray, and believe in the working of the Holy Spirit until we really see the Master in that special light in which the Word has been setting Him before us. Only then will we carry away the deep and abiding impression of that heavenly beauty in Him which we know is to be reproduced in us. Let us gaze, and gaze again, let us worship and adore; the more we see Him as He is, the more like Him we will become. To study the image of God in the man Christ Jesus, to yield ourselves for that image to take possession and live in us, and then to go forth and allow the heavenly likeness to reflect itself and shine out in our life among our fellowmen—*this is what we have been redeemed for; let this be what we live for.*

I have committed this book to the gracious care of the blessed Lord of whose glory it seeks to tell. May He cause us to see that there is no beauty or blessedness like that of a Christlike life. May He teach us to believe that in union with Him, the Christlike life is indeed for us. And as we daily listen to what His Word tells us of His image, may each one of us have grace to say, "O my Father! even as your beloved Son lived in you, with you, for you on earth, even so would I also live."

Andrew Murray
Wellington
Cape of Good Hope

1

Because We Abide in Him

"He that saith he abideth in him, ought himself also so to walk, even as he walked" (1 John 2:6).

Abiding in Christ and *walking like Christ*—these are the two blessings of the new life which are before us in their essential unity. The fruit of a life *in Christ* is a life *like Christ*.

The first expression, *abiding in Christ,* is no stranger to us. The parable of the Vine and the Branches, with the accompanying command, "Abide in me, and I in you," has often been a source of rich instruction and comfort to us. And though we may not have fully learned the lesson of abiding in Him, yet we have tasted something of the joy that comes when the soul can say: "Lord, you know that I do abide in you." And He knows, too, how often the fervent prayer still arises: "Blessed Lord, grant me unbroken abiding."

The second expression, *walking like Christ,* is no less significant. It is the promise of the wonderful power that abiding in Him will exert. As the fruit of our surrender to live wholly in Him, His life works so mightily in us that our walk, the outward expression of the inner life, becomes like His. The two are inseparably connected. Abiding always precedes walking. And yet the goal to walk like Him must equally precede any large measure of abiding. Only then is the need for a close union fully realized, or the heavenly Giver free to bestow the fullness

13

of His grace, because He sees that the soul is prepared to use it according to His design. When the Savior said, "If ye keep my commandments, ye shall abide in my love," He meant just this: the surrender to walk like Me is the path to the full abiding in Me. Many will discover that this is the secret of their failure in abiding in Christ: they did not seek it with the view of walking like Christ. The words of John invite us to look at the two truths in their vital connection and dependence on each other.

The first lesson they teach is: He that seeks to abide in Christ *must walk even as He walked*. We all know that a branch bears the same fruit as the vine to which it belongs. The life of the vine and the branch is so completely indentical that the manifestation of that life must be identical. When the Lord Jesus redeemed us with His blood, and presented us to the Father in His righteousness, He did not leave us unchanged to serve God as best we could. No; in Him dwelt eternal life, the divine life of heaven; and everyone who is in Him receives from Him that same eternal life in its holy heavenly power. Thus, nothing can be more natural than the claim that he who abides in Him, continually receiving life from Him, must *also so* walk *even as He* walked.

This mighty life of God in the soul does not, however, work as a blind force compelling us ignorantly or involuntarily to act like Christ. On the contrary, the walking like Him must come as the result of a deliberate choice, sought in strong desire, accepted by our will. The Father has shown us in Jesus' earthly life what the life of heaven would be when it came down into the conditions and circumstances of our human life. The Lord Jesus ever points us to His own life on earth, and tells us that the new life has been given to us to walk even as He walked. "Even as I, so ye also": that word of the Master takes His whole earthly life and makes it the rule and guide of all our conduct. If we abide in Jesus, we will live and act like He did. "Like Christ" gives in one short word the blessed law of the Christian life—he is to think, to speak, to act as Jesus did.

The second lesson is the complement of the first: He that seeks to walk like Christ *must abide in Him*.

There is a twofold need of this lesson. With some there is

the earnest desire and effort to follow Christ's example without any sense of the impossibility of doing so except by real abiding in Him. They fail because they seek to obey the high command to live like Christ without the only power that can do so—living in Christ. With others there is the opposite error: they know their own weakness and conclude walking like Christ is an impossibility. Both groups need the lesson we are enforcing. To walk like Christ one must abide in Him; he who abides in Him has the power to walk like Him—not indeed in himself or his own efforts, but in Jesus, who perfects His strength in our weakness. It is when I feel my utter inability most deeply, and fully accept Jesus in His wondrous union with me as my life, that His power works in me, and I am able to lead a life completely beyond what my power could obtain. I begin to see that abiding in Him is not a matter of brief encounters or special seasons, but the deep life process in which, by His keeping grace, I continue without a moment's intermission, and from which I live out all my Christian life. Therefore, I will not fear to take Him in everything as my example, because I am sure that the inner union and likeness must work itself out into a visible likeness in walk and conduct.

Dear believer, if God gives us grace to truly enter into the meaning of these His words and what they teach of a life like Christ's, we shall more than once come into the presence of heights and depths that will make us cry out, How can these things be? If the Holy Spirit reveals to us the heavenly perfection of the humanity of our Lord as the image of the unseen God, and speaks to us, "*So, even so* ought ye also to walk," the first effect will be that we will begin to feel we are so far from Him. We will be ready to give up hope, and to say with so many, There is no reason to attempt it; I can ever walk like Jesus. At such moments we shall find our strength in the message, *He that abideth in Him,* he must, he can, also walk even as He walked. The word of the Master will come with new meaning as the assurance of sufficient strength: "He that abideth in me beareth much fruit."

Therefore, abide in Him! Every believer is in Christ; but not everyone abides in Him in the consciously joyful and trustful surrender of the whole being to His influence. Abiding in Him is to consent with our whole soul to His being our life, to depend on Him to inspire us in all that we do, and to absolutely surrender everything for Him to rule and work in us. We rest in the full assurance that He works in us what we are to be and enables us to maintain that perfect surrender in which He is free to do all His will.

May all who desire to walk like Christ take courage in the thought of what He is and will prove himself to be if they trust Him. He is the *True Vine*. No vine has ever done for its branches what He will do for us. We have only to consent to be branches. Honor Him by a joyful trust that He is, beyond all conception, the *True Vine*, holding you by His almighty strength, supplying you from His infinite fullness. As your faith looks to Him, instead of sighing and failure, the voice of praise will be heard repeating the language of faith: Thanks be to God! he that abides in Him does walk even as He walked. Thanks be to God! I abide in Him and I walk as He walked. Yes, thanks be to God! in the blessed life of God's redeemed these two are inseparably one: abiding in Christ and walking like Christ.

Blessed Savior! you know how often I have said, I do abide in you! Yet I often sense a lack of joy and power of life. Your Word has reminded me of what may be the reason of failure. I sought to abide in you more for my own comfort and growth than for your glory. I failed to see that union with yourself had for its object perfect conformity to your image. Now I see that only those who wholly yield themselves to serve and obey the Father as you did can fully receive all that the heavenly love can do for him. And I see that the entire surrender to live and work like you must precede the full experience of the wondrous power of your life.

Lord, I thank you for this insight. With my whole heart I accept your word and yield myself in everything to walk *even as* you walked. To be your faithful follower in all I do is the one desire of my heart.

Blessed Lord! as I yield myself to walk as you walked, I also receive your abiding grace. Here I am. *To walk like Christ!* For this I do indeed consecrate myself. *To abide in Christ!* For this I trust in you with full assurance of faith. Perfect in me your own work.

And may the Holy Spirit help me. Each time I meditate on what it is to walk like you, to hold fast the truth that as one abides *in Christ*, I have the strength to walk *like Christ*. Amen.

2

He Himself Calls Us

"I have given you an example, that ye also should do as I have done to you" (John 13:15).

It is Jesus Christ, our beloved Redeemer, who spoke these words. He had just washed His disciples' feet, doing the work of a slave. His love had rendered to the physical body the service of which it stood in need at the supper table. At the same time He had shown, in a striking symbol, what He would do for their souls in cleansing them from sin. In this twofold work of love, He set before them the whole work of His life as a ministry of blessing to body and to soul. And as He sits down He says: "I have given you an example, that ye also should do as I have done to you." All they had seen in Him and experienced from Him is thus made the rule of their life.

The word of the blessed Savior is also for us. To all His redeemed the command comes with all the touching force of one of the last words of Him who is going out to die for us: "As I have done to you, so do ye also." Jesus Christ asks each of us in every situation of life to act just as we have seen Him do. What He has done to us, and still does each day, we are to do over again to others. In His condescending, pardoning, saving love, He is our example; each of us is to be the copy and image of the Master.

The thought comes at once: How little I have lived like Him!

I had not known that I was expected to so live! And yet, He is my lord; He loves me, and I love Him; I dare not entertain the thought of living other than He would have me. What can I do but open my heart to His Word and fix my gaze on His example, until it exercises its divine power upon me, and causes me to cry, "Lord, even as you were, so will I be!"

The power of an example depends primarily on two things: (1) the attractiveness of what it gives us to see; (2) the personal relation and influence of him in whom it is seen. In both aspects, what power there is in our Lord's example!

Yet, one wonders if there really is anything very attractive in our Lord's example. To judge by the conduct of many of His disciples, it would seem as if it were not. Oh, that the Spirit of God would open our eyes to see the heavenly beauty of the likeness of the only-begotten Son!

We know who the Lord Jesus is. He is the Son of the all-glorious God, one with the Father in nature and glory and perfection. When He had been on earth it could be said of Him, "We show unto you that eternal life, which was with the Father, and was manifested unto us" (1 John 1:20). In Him we see God. In Him we see how God would act were He here on earth. In Him is all that is beautiful and lovely and perfect in the heavenly world. If we would see what is really divine, we have only to look at Jesus; in all He does, the glory of God is demonstrated.

Such glory stands in contrast to the blindness of God's children; to many, this heavenly beauty apparently has no attractions; there is little in it that they seem to desire.

The manners and the way of living in the court of an earthly king exercise influence throughout the empire. The example it gives is imitated by all who belong to the nobility or the higher classes. But the example of the King of heaven, who came and dwelt in the flesh that we might see how to live a godlike life, alas! with how few of His followers does it find imitation. When we look at Jesus, His obedience to the will of the Father, His humiliation to be a servant of the most unworthy, His love as manifested in the entire surrender and sacrifice of himself, we see the most wondrous and glorious thing heaven has to show. Surely such an example ought to win us. Does it not stir all that is within us with a holy jealousy and with joy unutterable as we hear the message, "I have given you an example, that even as I have done, ye should also do"?

This is not all. The power of an example consists not only in its own intrinsic excellence but also in the personal relation to him who gives it. Jesus had not washed the feet of others in the presence of His disciples; it was when He had washed *their feet* that He said: "As I have done *to you*, ye should do." It is the consciousness of a personal relationship to Christ that enforces the command: Do as I have done. It is the experience of what Jesus had done for me that is the strength in which I can go and do the same to others. He does not ask that I do more than has been done to me. But not less either: as I have done to you. He does not ask that I shall humble myself as a servant deeper than He has done. It would not have been strange if He had asked this of such a worm. But this is not His wish: He only demands that I do and be what He, the King, has done and been. He humbled himself as low as humiliation could go, to love and to bless me. He counted this *His highest honor and blessedness.* And now He invites me to partake of the same honor and blessedness, in loving and serving as He did. If I truly know the love that rests on me, and the humiliation through which alone that love could reach me, and the power of the cleansing which has washed me, nothing can keep me back: "I will also do." The heavenly loveliness of the great example, and the divine lovingness of the great Exemplar, combine to make the example above everything attractive.

Only there is one thing I must not forget. It is not the remembrance of what Jesus has once done to me, but the living experience of what He is *now* to me, that will give me the power to act like Him. His love must be a present reality, the inflowing of a life and a power in which I can love like Him. It is only through the Holy Spirit that I realize *what* Jesus is doing for me, and *how* He does it, and that it is *He* who does it. Then it is possible for me to do to others what He is doing to me.

"As I have done to you, do ye also!" What a precious word! What a glorious prospect! Jesus is going to demonstrate in me the divine power of His love that others may see it. He blesses me that I may bless others. He loves me that I may love others. He becomes a servant to me that I may become a servant to others. He gives himself wholly for and to me that I may wholly give myself for and to others. I have only to be doing to others what He is doing to me—nothing more. I can do it just because He is doing it to me. What I do is nothing but repeating, demonstrating what I am receiving from Him.

It is His wondrous grace that calls us and enables us to be like our Lord. Shall not our whole heart joyously respond to His command? Yes, blessed Lord! even as you do to me so I also will do to others.

Gracious Lord, what can I now do but praise and pray? My heart is overwhelmed with this wondrous offer, that you will reveal all your love and power in me if I will yield myself to let it flow through me to others. With fear and trembling, in deep and grateful adoration, with joy and confidence, I accept the offer and say, Here I am; show me how much you love me, and I will show it to others by loving them.

Enable me to do this, blessed Lord. Grant me, by the Holy Spirit, a clear insight into your love for me that I may know how you love me, how your love for me is your delight and blessedness, how in that love you give yourself so completely to me that you are mine to do for me all I need. Grant this, Lord, and I shall know how to love and how to live for others.

And then grant me to see, as often as I feel how little love I have, that it is not with the love of my little heart, but with your love shed abroad in me, that I have to fulfill the command of loving like you. Am I not your branch, O my heavenly Vine? It is the fullness of your life and love that flows through me in love and blessing to those around. It is your Spirit that, at the same moment, reveals what you are to me, and strengthens me for what I am to be to others in your name. In this faith I dare to say, Amen, Lord, even as you do to me, I also do. Yea, Amen.

3

As One That Serves

"If I then, your Lord and Master, have washed your feet; ye also ought to wash one another's feet" (John 13:14).
"I am among you as he that serveth" (Luke 22:27).

In the previous chapter it was maintained that the Lord expects His redeemed ones to follow His example. In this chapter we will consider the way we are to follow Him.

"Ye also ought to wash one another's feet" is the phrase we want to study. Here we consider three primary thoughts: the *form* of a servant in which we see Him, the *cleansing* which was the object of *that* service, and the *love* which was its motive power.

First, the form of a servant. All was ready for the last supper, even the water to wash the feet of the guests, according to custom. But there was no slave to do the work. Each was waiting for the other: none of the twelve thought of humbling himself to do the work. Even at the table their thoughts were on which of them was greatest in the kingdom (Luke 22:24). Then Jesus rose (they were still reclining at the table), laid aside His garments, girded himself with a towel, and began to wash their feet. Such a wondrous spectacle on which angels gazed with adoring wonder! Christ, the Creator and King of the universe, whom legions of angels are ready to serve—Christ chose the slave's place for His own, took the soiled feet in His hands, and washed them. He did it in full consciousness of His role as redeemer, for John said, "Jesus knowing that the Father had given all things into his hands, and that he was come from God and went to God; he riseth" (John 13:3). For the hands into which God had given all things, nothing was common or unclean. Society's evaluation of the position of a work never lowers the person; the person honors and elevates the work, and imparts his own worth even to what is shunned as a slave's duty.

In such deep humiliation our Lord finds divine glory, and is in this the *leader* of His church in the path of true blessedness. Though He is the beloved of His Father, into whose hands all things are given, it is not difficult for Him to stoop so low. In thus taking the form of a servant, Jesus proclaims the law of rank in the Church of Christ. The higher one wishes to stand in grace, the more it must be his joy to be servant of all. "Whosoever will be chief among you, let him be your servant" (Matt. 20:27); "He that is greatest among you shall be your servant" (Matt. 23:11). The more I become like Christ, the deeper shall I stoop to serve all around me.

A servant is one who is always caring for the work and interest of his master, is ever ready to let his master see that he only seeks to do what will please or profit him. Thus Jesus lived: "For even the Son of man came not to be ministered unto, but to minister, and to give his life a ransom for many" (Mark 10:45); "I am among you as he that serveth." Thus I must live, moving among God's children as the servant of all. If I seek to bless others, it must be in the humble, loving readiness with which I serve them, not caring for my own honor or interest. I must follow Christ's example in washing the disciples' feet. A servant counts it no humiliation and is not ashamed of being an inferior: it is his position to serve others. The reason we so often do not bless others is that we wish to address them as their superiors in grace or gifts, or at least their equals. What a blessing we could be to the world if we learned from our Lord to associate with others in the blessed spirit of a servant. Were this example permitted to take its position in the Church of Christ, the power of His presence would soon make itself felt.

And what is our work as disciples in this spirit of lowly

service? The foot washing speaks of a double work—the one, for the cleansing and refreshing of the body; the other, the cleansing and saving of the soul. During our Lord's entire earthly ministry these two things were ever united: "The sick were healed, to the poor the gospel was preached." As with the paralytic, so with many others, blessing to the body was the type and promise of life to the spirit.

The follower of Jesus has received the command, "Ye ought also to wash one another's feet." Remembering that the external and bodily is the gate to the inner and spiritual life, he seeks to have a balanced ministry of love—seeking the way to the salvation of men's hearts by the ready service of love in the little and common things of daily life. It is not by reproof and rebuke that he shows he is a servant; no, but by the friendliness and kindness with which he proves in daily interaction that he is always there to be a help or to serve. He becomes the living witness of what it is to be a follower of Jesus. From such a one the word when spoken comes with power and finds easy entrance. And then when he comes into contact with the sin and perverseness of men, instead of being discouraged, he perseveres as he realizes how much patience Jesus has borne with him, and still daily cleanses him. He realizes himself to be one of God's appointed servants, to stoop to the lowest depth to serve and save men, even to bow at the feet of others if this be needed.

The spirit to live such a life of loving service can be learned from Jesus alone. John writes, "Having loved his own which were in the world, he loved them unto the end" (John 13:1). Nothing is too hard for love. Love never speaks of sacrifice. To bless the loved one, however unworthy, it willingly gives up all. Love made Jesus a servant. Love alone will make the servant's place and work such blessedness to us that we shall persevere in it at all costs. We may perhaps, like Jesus, have to wash the feet of some Judas who rewards us with ingratitude and betrayal. We shall probably meet many a Peter, who first, with his "never my feet," refuses, and then is dissatisfied when we do not comply with his impatient "not only the feet, but also the head and the hands." Only love, a heavenly unquenchable love, gives the patience, the courage, and the wisdom for this great work of which the Lord is our example: "Wash ye one another's feet."

Ask God for understanding on this: it is only as a son that you can truly be a servant. It was as the Son Christ took the form of a servant: in this you will find the secret of willing, happy service. Walk among men *as a son of the Most High God.* A son of God is only in the world to demonstrate His Father's glory, to prove how godlike and how blessed it is to live only and at any cost to find a way to the hearts of the lost.

Neither our soul nor our personal love can attain to this; therefore listen to Him who says, "Abide in *my love.*" Our one desire must be to receive His love and then to abide in *"His love."* Live every day, as the beloved of the Lord, in the consciousness that His love washes and cleanses, strengthens and blesses you all the day long. His love flowing into you will flow out again from you and make it your greatest joy to follow His example in washing the feet of others. Do not complain about the lack of love and humility in others, but pray much that the Lord would awaken His people to their calling as servants. Only as we follow in His footsteps will the world see Christ as He really is. And if you do not see it as soon as you wish in those around you, let it only urge you to more earnest prayer, that at least in you the Lord may have one who understands and proves that to love and serve like Jesus is the highest blessedness and joy, as well as the way, like Jesus, to be a blessing and a joy to others.

My Lord, I give myself to you, to live this blessed life of serving. I have seen that your spirit of serving is a kingly spirit, come from heaven and lifting up to heaven. How little my heart has resembled this, the Spirit of God's own Son. Everlasting love, come dwell in me, and my life shall be like yours, and the language of my life to others shall become, "I am in the midst of you as he that serveth."

Glorified Son of God, you know how this life of a servant is opposed to all that the world considers honorable or proper. But you have come to teach us what is right, to show us what is thought in heaven of the glory of being the least, of the blessedness of serving. Yet, you do not only give us new thoughts but implant new feelings; so give me a heart like yours, a heart full of the Holy Spirit, a heart that can love as you do. Your Holy Spirit dwells within me; your fullness is my inheritance; in the joy of the Holy Spirit I can be as you are. I do yield myself to a life of service like yours. May my mind become like yours— when you made yourself of no reputation, the form of a servant, and being found in fashion as a man, did humble yourself. By your grace, as a son of God, let me be the servant of men. Amen.

4

Our Head

"For even hereunto were ye called; because Christ also suffered for us, leaving us an example, that ye should follow his steps: who his own self bare our sins in his own body on the tree, that we being dead to sins, should live unto righteousness" (1 Pet. 2:21, 24).

The call to follow Christ's example and to walk in His footsteps is absolutely clear. Yet, one wonders how it can be expected that sinful men should walk like the Son of God. The answer most people give is that it cannot really be expected: the command sets before us an ideal, beautiful but unattainable.[1]

The answer Scripture gives is different. It points us to the wonderful relationship in which we stand to Christ. Union with Him sets in operation within us the divine life with all its powers; therefore, the claim may be made that we should live as Christ did. The realization of this relationship is the key to following Christ's example.

This relationship is threefold. Peter speaks in this passage of Christ as our *Surety*, our *Example*, and our *Head*.

Christ is our *Surety*. "Christ suffered *for us*"—"who his own self *bare our sins* in his own body on the tree." As surety, Christ

---

[1]See the note at the end of the chapter.

suffered and died in our place. He bore our sin and broke its curse and power. As surety, He did what we could not do, what we now need not do.

Christ is also our *Example*. In one sense His work is unique; in another, we are to follow Him in it. "Christ *suffered for us, leaving us an example*" that we should follow in His footsteps. His suffering as my surety calls me to a suffering like His as my example. But is this reasonable? Can I be expected in the weakness of the flesh to suffer as He did? Is there an impassable gulf between these two things which Peter unites so closely, the suffering as surety and the suffering as example? No, there is a blessed third aspect of Christ's work which bridges that gulf, which is the connecting link between Christ as surety and Christ as example, and makes it possible for us to live and suffer and die like Him.

Christ is also our *Head*. In this His suretyship and His example have their root and unity. Christ is the second Adam. As a believer I am spiritually one with Him. In this union He lives in me, and imparts to me the power of His finished work, the power of His sufferings and death and resurrection. It is on this ground we are taught in Romans 6 and elsewhere that the Christian is indeed dead to sin and alive to God. The very life that Christ lives, the life that passed through death, and the power of that death, work in the believer, so that he is dead and has risen again with Christ. It is this thought that Peter expresses when he says: "Who his own self bore our sins upon the tree," not only that we through His death might receive forgiveness, but "that we, being *dead to sins, should live* unto righteousness." As we have part in the spiritual death of the first Adam, having really died to God, so we have part in the second Adam, having really died to sin in Him, and in Him being made alive again to God. Christ is not only our surety who lived and died for us, our example who showed us how to live and die, but also our head with whom we are one—in whose death we have died, and with whose life we now live. This gives us the power to follow our surety as our example: Christ being our head is the bond that makes the believing on the surety and the following of the example inseparably one.

These three truths are one and may not be separated from each other. And yet this happens too often. Some wish to follow Christ's example without faith in His atonement. They seek within themselves the power to live like Him; their efforts must be vain. Others hold fast to the suretyship but neglect the example. They believe in redemption through the blood of the cross, but neglect the footsteps of Him who bore it. Faith in the atonement is indeed the foundation of the building, but it is not all. Theirs is a deficient Christianity with no understanding of sanctification. They do not see that faith in Christ's atonement involves following His example.

There are still others who have received these two truths— Christ as surety and Christ as example—and still are lacking. They feel constrained to follow Christ as example in what He did as surety, but lack power. They do not understand how this can be attained. What they need is clear insight as to what Scripture teaches of Christ as head. Because the surety is not someone outside of me, but One in whom I am and who is in me, I can become like Him. His very life lives in me; He himself lives in me. To follow His footsteps is a duty because it is a possibility, the natural result of the wonderful union between Head and members. It is only when this is understood that the blessed truth of Christ's example will take its place. If Jesus himself through His life-union will work in me the life-likeness, then my duty becomes plain, but glorious. I have, on the one side, to gaze on His example so as to know and follow it; on the other, to abide in Him and open my heart to the blessed workings of His life in me. As surely as He conquered sin and its curse *for me* will He conquer sin's power *in me*. What He began by His death for me, He will perfect by His life in me. Because my surety is also my head, His example must and will be the rule of my life.

There is a saying of Augustine that is often quoted: "Lord! give what Thou commandest, and command what Thou wilt." This holds true here. If the Lord, who lives in me, *gives* what He requires of me, then no requirement can be too high. Then I have the courage to gaze upon His holy example in all its height and breadth, and to accept it as the rule for my conduct.

It is no longer simply a command telling what I must be, but a promise of what I shall be. There is nothing that weakens the power of Christ's example as much as the lie that we cannot really walk like Him. Do not listen to such thoughts. The perfect likeness in heaven is begun on earth, can grow with each day, and becomes more visible as life goes on. As certain and powerful as the work of surety which Christ completed once for all is the renewal after His own image which He is still working out. Let this double blessing make the cross doubly precious: Our head suffered as a surety that in union with us He might bear sin for us. Our head suffered as an example that He might show us the path in which, in union with himself, He would lead us to victory and glory. The suffering Christ is our *Head*, our *Surety*, and our *Example*.

The great lesson to learn is that it is in that mysterious path of suffering, in which He accomplished our atonement and redemption, that we are to follow His footsteps, and that the full experience of that redemption depends upon the personal fellowship in that suffering. "Christ suffered for us, leaving us an example." May the Holy Spirit reveal to us what this means.

Precious Savior, how shall I thank you for the work you have done as surety? Standing in the place of me, a guilty sinner, you bore my sins in your body on the cross. That cross was my due. You took it—all the sin and suffering—that the cross might be changed into a place of blessing and life.

You have called me to the place of crucifixion as the place of blessing and life, where I may be made like you and may find power to suffer and to cease from sin. As my head, you were my surety to suffer and die with me; as my head, you are my example that I might suffer and die with you.

Precious Savior, I confess my lack of understanding this. Your suretyship has been more to me than your example. I rejoiced much that you bore the cross for me, but too little that I might follow in your footsteps. The atonement of the cross was more precious to me than the fellowship of the cross; the hope in your redemption more precious than the personal fellowship with you.

Forgive me, dear Lord, and teach me to find my happiness in union with you, my head, not more in your suretyship than in your example. And grant that as I seek how to follow you, my faith may become stronger and brighter: Jesus is my example because He is my life. I must and can be like Him because I am one with Him. Grant this, my blessed Lord, for your love's sake. Amen.

NOTE

"Thomas à Kempis has said, 'All men wish to be with Christ, and to belong to His people; but few are really willing to follow the life of Christ.' There are many who imagine that to imitate Jesus Christ is a specially advanced state in the Christian life, to which only a few elect can attain; they think that one can be a real Christian if he only confesses his weakness and sin, and holds fast to the Word and Sacrament, *without attaining any real conformity to the life of Christ;* they even count it pride and fanaticism if one venture to say *that conformity to the likeness of Jesus Christ is an indispensable sign of the true Christian.* And yet our Lord says to all without exception: 'He that doth not take his cross, and follow after me, is not worthy of me.' He mentions expressly the most difficult thing in His life— the cross, that which includes all else. And Peter writes not to some, but to the whole Church: Christ hath left us an example that ye should follow His footsteps. It is a sad sign that these unmistakable commands have been so darkened in our modern Christianity that our leading ministers and church members have quietly, as by common consent, agreed to rob these words of their sting.

"A false dogmatic must bear no small share of the blame. To defend the divinity of our Savior against unbelief, men have presented and defended His divine nature with such exclusiveness that it became impossible to form any real living conception of His humanity. It is not enough that we admit Christ was a true man; no one can form any true idea of this humanity who is ever afraid to lose the true Christ if he does not every moment ascribe to Him divine power and omniscience. For, of a truth, if Christ's suffering and cross be only and altogether something supernatural, we must cease to speak of the imitation of Christ in any true or real sense of the word. Oh, the gulf of separation which comes between the life of Christ and the life of Christians when the relation between them is only an external one! And how slow and slothful the Church of our days is to apply the great and distinct rule so clearly laid down in the life of Christ, to the filling of these gulfs and the correction of the disorders of our modern life. The Church of Christ will not be brought again out of its confusions until *the faithful actual imitation of her Lord and Head again become the banner round which she rallies His disciples.*"[2]

---

[2]From M. Diemer, *Een nieuw boek over de navolging van Jesus Christus* (a book on the imitation of Jesus Christ).

5

In Suffering Wrong

"For this is thankworthy, if a man for conscience toward God endure grief, suffering wrongfully. For what glory is it, if, when ye be buffeted for your faults, ye shall take it patiently? but if, when ye do well, and suffer for it, ye take it patiently, this is acceptable with God" (1 Pet. 2:19, 20).

It is in connection with a servant or slave's role that Peter wrote these weighty words concerning Christ as our *surety* and *example*. He teaches them "to be subject with all," not only to the good and gentle, but also to the adverse (2:18). He writes that if they are punished for doing wrong, to bear it patiently is no special grace. But, if they have done well and still suffer for it, and take it patiently, this is acceptable with God; such bearing of wrong is Christlike. In bearing our sins as surety, Christ suffered wrong from man; following His example we must be ready to suffer wrongfully too.

It is extremely difficult to bear injustice from others. It is not only the loss we suffer—there is the *feeling* of humiliation and injustice, and the *consciousness* of our rights asserting themselves. Caught up in the injustice, it is difficult to recognize the will of God, who allows us to be tried and proven concerning our likeness to His example. Let us study that example. From Him we discover the power to bear injuries patiently.

Christ believed in suffering as the will of God. He had found it in Scripture that the servant of God would suffer. He made himself familiar with the thought, so that when suffering came, it did not take Him by surprise. He expected it. He knew that this was God's method to bring Him to perfection; and so His first thought was not how to be delivered from it, but how to glorify God in it. This enabled Him to bear the greatest injustice quietly. He saw God's hand in it.

Here is a secret to the spiritual strength that willingly suffers wrong: accustom yourself in everything that happens to recognize the hand and will of God. Whether it be some great wrong that is done you, or some little offense that you meet in daily life, before you consider the person who did it, first be still and remember, *God allows me to come into this trouble to see if I will glorify Him in it.* This trial, be it great or small, is allowed by God and is His will concerning me. Let me first recognize and submit to *God's will* in it. Then with the peace of God which this gives, I will receive wisdom to know how to behave in it. With my eye turned from man to God, suffering wrong takes on this new dimension.

Christ believed that God would care for His rights and honor. There is an inborn sense of right within us that comes from God. That does not mean, however, that we were meant to vindicate our personal honor. Jesus saw beyond the temporal injustice and was satisfied to leave the vindication of His rights and honor in God's hands; He knew they were safe with Him. Peter writes, "He committed himself to him that judgeth righteously" (2:23). It was settled between the Father and the Son: the Son was not to care for His own honor, but only for the Father's. The Father would care for the Son's honor. Let the believer follow Christ's example in this; it will give him such rest and peace. Commit your right and your honor into God's keeping. Meet every offense that man commits against you with the firm trust that God will watch over and care for you.

Further, *Christ believed in the power of suffering love.* We all admit there is no power like that of love. Through it Christ overcomes the enmity of the world. Every other type of victory gives only a forced submission; love alone gives the true victory over an enemy by transforming him into a friend. We all ac-

knowledge this truth as a principle, but we fail in its application. Christ believed it, and acted accordingly. He said too, I
shall have my revenge; but His revenge was that of love, bringing enemies as friends to His feet. He believed that by silence
and submission, and suffering and bearing wrong, He would
win the cause, because through it love would have its triumph.

And this is what He desires of us. We have more faith in
might and right than in the heavenly power of love. But if we
desire to follow Christ, we, too, must conquer evil with good.
*The more another does us wrong, the more we should feel called
to love him.* Even if it is necessary for the public welfare that
justice should punish the offender, care is taken so that there
is nothing of personal feeling in it; as far as we are concerned,
he is forgiven and loved.

What a difference it would make in our churches if Christ's
example were followed! If each one who was reviled "reviled not
again"; if each one who suffered "threatened not, but committed
himself to him that judgeth righteously." This is literally what
the Father would have us do. Read and read again the words
of Peter until your soul is filled with the thought, "If, when ye
do well, and suffer for it, ye take it patiently, *this is acceptable
with God.*"[1]

If we are still seeking to fulfill our calling in our own
strength, such a conformity to the Lord's image is an impossibility. But in a life of full surrender, where we have given all
our rights to Him, faith will work in us the imitation of His
willingness to suffer. And accompanying this imitation is the
glorious promise: "Christ also suffered for us, so that we, being
dead to sins, might live unto righteousness."

It is our highest privilege to become like Jesus, and in bearing injuries to act as He himself would act in our place. For our
strength it is too high; in His strength it is possible. Only surrender yourself to God daily to be in all things just what He
would have you to be. Believe that He lives in heaven to be the
life and the strength of each one who seeks to walk in His
footsteps. Yield yourself to be one with the suffering, crucified

---

[1]See the note at the end of the chapter.

Christ, that you may understand what it is to be dead to sins and to live unto righteousness. It will be your joy to experience the power in Jesus' death to break sin's dominion; and in His resurrection to make you live unto righteousness. You will find it *equally blessed to follow fully the footsteps of the suffering Savior* as it has been to trust fully and only in that suffering for atonement and redemption. Christ will be as precious as your *example* as He has ever been as your *surety*. Because He took your sufferings upon himself, you will lovingly take His sufferings upon yourself. And bearing wrong will become a glorious part of the fellowship with His holy sufferings; a glorious mark of being conformed to His most holy likeness; a most blessed fruit of the true life of faith.

Lord, your word is precious: If any man endure grief, suffering wrongfully, and take it patiently this is acceptable with God. This is indeed a sacrifice that is well-pleasing to you, a work that your grace alone has accomplished, a fruit of the suffering of your beloved Son, of the example He left, and the power He gives in virtue of His having destroyed the power of sin.

Father, teach me to aim at nothing less than complete conformity to your dear Son's image. I would now, once for all, surrender my honor and my rights into your hands, never again to take charge of them. You will care for them most perfectly. May my only care be the honor and the rights of my Lord!

I especially ask you to fill me with faith in the conquering power of suffering love. Cause me to fully understand how the suffering Lamb of God teaches us that patience and silence and suffering avail more with you, and therefore with man too, than might or right. Oh, my Father, I must, I will walk in the footsteps of my Lord Jesus. Let your Holy Spirit and the light of your love and presence be my guide and strength. Amen.

NOTE

"What is it thou sayest, my son? Cease from complaining, when thou considerest my passion, and the sufferings of my other saints. Do not say, 'To suffer this from such a one, it is more than I can or may do. He has done me great wrong, and accused me of things I never thought of. Of another I might bear it, if I thought I deserved it, but not from him!' Such thoughts are very foolish; instead of thinking of patience in suffering, or of Him by whom it will be crowned, we only are occupied with the injury done to us, and the person who has done it. No, he deserves not the name of patient *who is only willing to suffer as much as he thinks proper, and from whom he pleases.* The truly patient man asks not from whom he suffers—his superior, his equal, or his inferior; whether from a good and holy man, or one who is perverse and unworthy. But from whomsoever, how much soever, or how often soever wrong is done him, he accepts it all and counts it gain. For with God it is impossible that anything suffered for His sake should pass without its reward.

"O Lord, let that become possible to me by your grace, which by nature seems impossible. Grant that the suffering wrong may by your love be made pleasant to me. To suffer for your sake is most healthful to my soul."[2]

---

[2]From Thomas à Kempis, *Of the Imitation of Christ*, iii. 19.

6

Crucified with Him

*"I am crucified with Christ: nevertheless I live; yet not I, but
Christ liveth in me. God forbid that I should glory, save in the
cross of our Lord Jesus Christ, by whom the world is crucified
unto me, and I unto the world"* (Gal. 2:20; 6:14).

Taking up the cross was always spoken of by Christ as the
test of discipleship. On three different occasions (Matt. 10:38;
16:24; Luke 14:27), we find the words repeated, "If any man
will come after me, let him deny himself and take up his cross
and follow me." While the Lord was on His way to the cross,
this expression—taking up the cross—was clearly defined as to
the conformity to which the disciple is called.[1] But now that He
has been crucified, the Holy Spirit gives another expression in
which our entire conformity to Christ is still more powerfully
set forth: the believer is crucified *with* Christ. The cross is the
chief mark of both the believer and Christ; the crucified Christ
and the crucified believer belong to each other. One of the chief
elements of likeness to Christ is that of being crucified with
Him. Whoever desires to be like Him must seek to understand
the secret of fellowship with His cross.

The believer who is seeking conformity to Jesus is usually
initially afraid of this truth; he shrinks from the painful suf-

---

[1]See the note at the end of the chapter.

fering and death with which the cross is connected. As his spiritual discernment becomes clearer, however, this word becomes his hope and joy, and he glories in the cross because it makes him a partner in a death and victory that has already been accomplished, and in which the deliverance from the powers of the flesh and of the world has been secured to him. To understand this we must notice carefully the language of Scripture.

"I am crucified with Christ," Paul says; "nevertheless I live; yet not I, but Christ liveth in me." Through faith in Christ we become partakers of Christ's life. That life has passed through the death of the cross, and *in it the power of that death is always working.* When I receive that life, I receive the full power of the death on the cross working in me in its never-ceasing energy. "I am crucified with Christ; nevertheless I live; yet not I, but Christ liveth in me." The life I now live is not my own life, but the life of the crucified One, the life of the cross. Being crucified is past and done: "We know that our old self *was* crucified with him" (Rom. 6:6, RSV); "They that are Christ's *have* crucified the flesh" (Gal. 5:24). "Far be it from me to glory except in the cross of our Lord Jesus Christ, by which the world *has been* crucified to me, and I to the world" (Gal. 6:14, RSV). These texts speak of something that *has been done* in Christ and into which I come by faith.

It is of great consequence to understand this, and to testify to the truth: I have been crucified with Christ; I have crucified the flesh. It is here I learn to share in the finished work of Christ. If I am crucified and dead with Him, then I am a partner in His life and victory. Only here will the power of that cross and death manifest itself in mortifying or putting to death the old man and the flesh, in destroying the body of sin (Rom. 6:6).

We often misunderstand our role in this. It is not my work to crucify myself: I *have been* crucified; the old man *was* crucified, so the Scripture speaks. My place is to always regard and treat it as crucified, and not to allow it to come down from the cross. I must maintain my crucified position; I must keep the flesh in the place of crucifixion. To realize the force of this I must notice an important distinction. I have been crucified and am dead: the old man, or self, was crucified. When I gave myself to my crucified Savior, sin and flesh and all, He took me wholly up with Him in His crucifixion. But here a separation took place. In fellowship with Him I was freed from the old life; I myself died with Him; in the inmost center of my being I received new life: Christ lives in *me*. But the flesh, with its strong natural desires, in which I yet am, is not yet dead. It is my calling, in fellowship with and in the strength of my Lord, to see that the flesh is kept nailed to the cross. All its desires and affections cry out, "Come down from the cross; save yourself and us." It is my duty to glory in the cross, and with my whole heart to maintain the dominion of the cross, to make dead every uprising of sin, as already crucified, and so not to allow it to have dominion. This is what Scripture means when it says, "If by the Spirit you put to death the deeds of the body, you will live" (Rom. 8:13, RSV). "Put to death therefore what is earthly in you" (Col. 3:5, RSV). Thus I continually acknowledge that in my flesh dwells no good thing; that my Lord is Christ the crucified One; that I have been crucified and *am dead* in Him; that the flesh has been crucified and, though not yet dead, has been forever given over to the death of the cross. And so I live like Christ, in very deed crucified with Him.

Two things are especially necessary to those who are Christ's followers. The first is the clear consciousness of their fellowship with the crucified One through faith. At conversion they became partakers of it without fully understanding it. Many remain in this state of spiritual ignorance all their life. Do pray that the Holy Spirit will reveal your union to the crucified One. "I have been crucified with Christ"; "the cross of our Lord Jesus Christ, by whom the world is crucified unto me." Take such words of Scripture, and by prayer and meditation make them your own, with a heart that expects and asks the Holy Spirit to make them living and effectual within you. View yourself in the light of God as "crucified with Christ."

Then you will find the grace for the second thing you need. You will be able to always look upon and to treat the flesh and the world as nailed to the cross. The flesh seeks continually to assert itself and to make you feel that it is expecting too much to always live this crucified life. Your only safety is in fellowship with Christ. Through Him and His cross, says Paul, I have been crucified to the world. In Him the crucifixion is an accomplished reality; in Him you have died, but also have been made alive: Christ lives in you. As you allow this fellowship of His cross to be with you (the deeper the better), it will bring you into deeper communion with His life and His love. To be crucified with Christ means freedom from the power of sin: a redeemed one, a conqueror. Remember that the Holy Spirit has been provided to glorify and reveal Christ in you, and to make real in you what Christ has provided. Do not be satisfied to know the cross only in its power to forgive: know the power of the cross as the path to a life which destroys sin and death and keeps us in the power of the eternal life. Faith in the power of the cross and its victory will be the source of strength to crucify the deeds of the body, the lusts of the flesh. This faith will teach you to consider the cross, with its continual death to self, all your glory. Because you regard your crucifixion with Christ as in the past and are already alive in Christ, the cross becomes the blessed instrument through which the body of sin is done away (Rom. 6:6). The banner under which complete victory over sin and the world is to be won is the cross.

Above all, remember that it is Jesus, the living Savior, who himself enables you to be like Him in all things. His sweet fellowship, His tender love, His heavenly power, make it a blessedness and joy to be like Him, the crucified One. The crucified life is a life of resurrection-joy and power. *In Him* the two are inseparably connected. In Him you have the strength to be always singing the triumphant song: God forbid that I should glory save in the cross of our Lord Jesus Christ, through which the world has been crucified to me and I to the world.

Precious Savior, I humbly ask you to show me the hidden glory of the fellowship of your cross. The cross was my place, the place of death and curse. You became like us and have been crucified with us. And now the cross is your place of blessing and life. And you have called me to become like you, as one who is crucified with you, to experience how entirely the cross has made me free from sin.

Lord, help me to know its full power. I have long known the power of the cross to redeem from the curse. But I have striven in vain to overcome the power of sin, and to obey the Father as you did! I cannot break the power of sin. But now I see that this comes only when I surrender myself to be led by your Holy Spirit into the fellowship of your cross. Through the cross the power of sin *has been broken forever*, and I have been set free. There you impart to me your own Spirit of wholehearted self-sacrifice in casting out and conquering sin. Oh, my Lord, teach me to understand this better. In faith I say, "I have been crucified with Christ." You alone are the crucified One, the One whom I seek and in whom I hope. Take me, crucified One, and hold me fast, and teach me from moment to moment to look upon all that is of self as condemned and only worthy to be crucified. Take me, hold me, and teach me, from moment to moment, that in you I have all I need for a life of holiness and blessing. Amen.

NOTE

"Jesus hath now many lovers of His heavenly kingdom, but few bearers of His cross. He hath many who desire His consolation, few His tribulation; many who are willing to share His table, few His fasting. All are willing to rejoice with Him; few will endure anything for Him. Many follow Jesus into the breaking of bread, but few to drink of the cup whereof He drank. Many glory in His miracles, few in the shame of His cross."[2]

"To many it seems a hard speech, 'Deny thyself, take up thy cross, and follow Jesus.' But it will be much harder to hear that other word, 'Depart from me, ye cursed'; for only they who now hear and follow the word of the cross shall then have no fear of the word of condemnation. For the sign of the cross will be seen in the heaven when the Lord cometh to judgment, and all the servants of the cross, who in their lifetime have been conformed to Christ crucified, will then draw near to Christ their judge with great confidence. Why, then, dost thou fear to take up the

---

[2]From Thomas à Kempis, *Of the Imitation of Christ*, ii. 11.

cross which fitteth thee for the kingdom? In the cross is life, in the cross is salvation; the cross defends against all enemies; in the cross there is the infusion of all heavenly sweetness; in the cross is strength of mind, joy of spirit; the cross is the height of virtue and the perfection of sanctity. There is no happiness for the soul but in the cross. Take up, therefore, thy cross and follow Jesus, and thou shalt live forever.

"If thou bear the cross cheerfully, it will bear thee. If thou bear it unwillingly, thou makest for thyself a burden which still thou hast to bear. What saint was there ever who did not bear the cross? Even Christ must needs suffer. How then dost thou seek any other way than this, which is the royal way, the way of the sacred cross?

"He that willingly submits to the cross, to him its whole burden is changed into a sweet assurance of divine comfort. And the more the flesh is broken down by the cross, the more the spirit is strengthened by inward grace. It is not in man by nature to bear the cross, to love the cross, to deny self, to bring the body into subjection, and willingly to endure suffering. If thou look to thyself, thou canst accomplish nothing of all this. But if thou trust in the Lord, strength shall be given thee from heaven, and the world and the flesh shall be made subject to thy rule. Set thyself, therefore, to bear manfully the cross of thy Lord, who out of love was crucified for thee.

"Know for certain thou oughtest to lead a dying life, for the more any man dieth unto himself, the more he liveth unto God. Surely, if there had been any better things, and more profitable to man's salvation, than bearing the cross, Christ would have showed it us by word and example. But now He calleth all who would follow Him plainly to do this one thing, daily to bear the cross."[3]

---

[3]From Thomas à Kempis, *Of the Imitation of Christ*, ii 12.

7

In His Self-denial

"We then that are strong ought to bear the infirmities of the weak, and not to please ourselves. Let every one of us please his neighbor for his good to edification. For even Christ pleased not himself, as it is written, The reproaches of them that reproached thee fell on me. Wherefore receive ye one another, as Christ also received us to the glory of God" (Rom. 15:1–3, 7).

"If any man will come after me, let him deny himself, and take up his cross, and follow me" (Matt. 16:24).

Even Christ pleased not himself. He bore the reproaches, with which men reproached and dishonored God, so patiently that He might glorify God and save man. Christ pleased not himself: with reference both to God and man, this word is the key to understanding His life. In this, too, His life is our rule and example; we must not live to please ourselves.

To deny self is the opposite of pleasing self. When Peter denied Christ, he said: I know not the man; I have nothing to do with Him; I do not wish to be counted His friend. In the same way the believer denies himself, regarding the old life: I do not know this old man; I will have nothing to do with him and his interests. And when shame and dishonor come upon him, or something that is not pleasant to the old life, he simply says: Do as you want with the old man, I take no notice of it. Through the cross of Christ I am crucified to the world, the flesh, and

44

self; to the friendship and interest of this old man I am a stranger; I deny him to be my friend; I deny his every claim and desire; I know him not.

The believer who thinks of his salvation as only from condemnation cannot understand this; he finds it impossible to deny self. Although he may sometimes try to do so, his life mainly consists in pleasing himself. The believer who has taken Christ as his example cannot be content with this. He has surrendered himself to seek the most complete fellowship with the cross of Christ. The Holy Spirit has taught him to say, I have been crucified with Christ, and so am dead to sin and self. In fellowship with Christ he sees the old man crucified; he is ashamed to have him as a friend. It is his fixed purpose, and he has received the power for it, to no longer please his old self, but to deny it. *Because the crucified Christ is his life, self-denial is the law of his life.*

This self-denial extends into every area of his life. It was so with the Lord Jesus, and it is so with everyone who desires to follow Him perfectly. This self-denial has not so much to do with what is morally contrary to the laws of God as with what is lawful, or at least apparently neutral. To the self-denying spirit, the will and glory of God and the salvation of man are always more than our own interests or pleasure.

Before we can learn to please our neighbor, self-denial must first exercise itself in our own personal life. It must rule the physical body. During the forty-day fast, Jesus said, "Man shall not live by bread alone, but by every word that proceedeth out of the mouth of God" (Matt. 4:4). He would not eat until His Father gave Him food and His Father's work was done. Surely this teaches the believer a holy temperance in eating and drinking. Surely the lifestyle of Him who had no place to lay His head teaches the believer to regulate the possession, use, and enjoyment of earthly things that he may always possess as not possessing. Surely the suffering of Him who bore all our sins in His own body on the tree teaches the believer to bear all suffering patiently. Even in the body as the temple of the Holy Spirit, he desires to bear about the dying of the Lord Jesus. Paul spoke of bringing and keeping the body under subjection;

all its desires and appetites he would have ruled by the self-denial of Jesus. He does not please himself.

This self-denial keeps watch over the spirit too. His own wisdom and judgment the believer brings into subjection to God's Word; he gives up his own thoughts to the teaching of the Word and the Spirit. Toward man he manifests the same self-denial of his own wisdom in a readiness to hear and learn, in the meekness and humility with which, even when he knows he is right, he gives his opinion, in the desire to ever find and acknowledge what is good in others.

And the self-denial has special reference to the heart. All the affections and desires are placed under it. The will, the kingly power of the soul, is especially under its control. As little as self-pleasing influenced Christ's life, to the same measure should the believer allow it to influence his life. "We . . . ought . . . not to please ourselves. For even Christ pleased not himself." Self-denial is the law of his life.

The believer does not find this hard after he has truly surrendered himself to Christ. To one who, with a divided heart, seeks to force himself to a life of self-denial, it is hard indeed. But to one who has yielded himself to Christ unreservedly because he has with his whole heart accepted the cross to destroy the power of sin and self, the blessing it brings more than compensates for apparent sacrifice or loss. He hardly dares to call it self-denial; there is such blessedness in becoming conformed to the image of Jesus.

Self-denial is not valuable to God, as some think, from the measure of pain it causes. No, this pain is very much caused by the reluctance to practice it. But it has its highest worth in that meek or even joyful acquiescence which counts nothing a sacrifice for Jesus' sake, and feels surprised when others speak of self-denial.

There have been ages when men thought they must depart to the wilderness or cloister to deny themselves. Jesus has shown us that the best place to practice self-denial is in our ordinary lives with men. So Paul also says, *"We . . . ought . . . not to please ourselves,* let every one of us please his *neighbor to edification. For even Christ pleased not himself. . . .* Wherefore receive ye one another, *as Christ* also received us." Nothing less than the self-denial of our Lord, who pleased not himself, is our law. What He was we must be. What He did we must do.

How glorious the Church would be if this law would prevail! Every member considering it his reason for living to make others happy. Each one denying himself, seeking not his own, esteeming others better than himself. All thought of taking offense, of wounded pride, of being slighted or passed by disregarded. Followers of Christ seeking to bear the weak and to please his neighbor. True self-denial seen as no one thinking of himself, but living in and for others.

"If any man will *come after* me, let him deny himself, take up his cross, and *follow me*." This word not only gives us the will but also the power for self-denial. He who does not simply wish to reach heaven through Christ, but comes after him for His own sake, will *follow* Him. And in his heart Jesus takes the place that self had. *Jesus only* becomes the center and object of such a life. The undivided surrender to follow Him is crowned with this wonderful blessing, that Christ by His Spirit becomes his life. Christ's spirit of self-denying love is poured out upon him, and to deny self is the greatest joy of his heart, and the means of the deepest communion with God. Self-denial is no longer a work for attaining perfection for himself. Nor is it merely a negative victory, of which the main feature is keeping self in check. Christ has taken the place of self, and His love and gentleness and kindness flow out to others, now that self is crucified. No command becomes more blessed or more natural than this: *"We ought . . . not to please ourselves, for even Christ pleased not himself."* "If any man come after me, let him deny himself, and *follow me*."

Beloved Lord, I thank you for this call to follow you, and not to please myself, even as you did not please yourself. I thank you that I no longer have to hear it with fear. Your commandments are no longer grievous to me; your yoke is easy, and your burden light. I see in your life on earth the certain pledge of what I receive from your life in heaven. I did not always understand this. Long after conversion I dared not think of self-denial. But for him who has learned what it is to take up the cross, to be crucified with you, and to see the old man nailed to the cross, it is no longer terrible to deny it. Since I have learned that you are my life, and that you wholly take charge of the life that is wholly entrusted to you, to work both to will and to do, I do not fear. You give me the love and wisdom in the path of self-denial to joyfully follow your footsteps. Blessed Lord, I am not worthy of this grace; but since you have chosen me, I will gladly seek to not please myself but my neighbor, as you taught. And may your Holy Spirit work mightily in me. Amen.

8

In His Self-sacrifice

"Walk in love as Christ also hath loved us, and hath given himself for us an offering and a sacrifice to God for a sweet-smelling savor" (Eph. 6:2).

"Hereby perceive we the love of God, because he laid down his life for us: and we ought to lay down our lives for the brethren" (1 John 3:16).

What is the connection between self-sacrifice and self-denial? The former is the root from which the latter springs. In self-denial, self-sacrifice is tested, and thus strengthened and prepared each time again to renew its entire surrender. So it was with the Lord Jesus. His incarnation was a self-sacrifice; His life of self-denial was the proof of it; through this He was prepared for the great act of self-sacrifice in His death on the cross. The same is true with the believer. His conversion is to a certain extent the sacrifice of self, perhaps a partial one due to ignorance and weakness. From that first act of self-surrender arises the obligation to the exercise of daily self-denial. The believer's efforts to do so show him his weakness, and prepare him for that new and more entire self-sacrifice in which he first finds strength for more continuous self-denial.

Self-sacrifice is of the very essence of true love. The very nature and blessedness of love consists in forgetting self and seeking its happiness in the loved one. Where there is a want or need in the beloved, love is impelled by its very nature to offer up its own happiness for that of the other, to unite itself to the beloved one, and at any sacrifice to make him the sharer of its own blessedness.

Sin's entrance into the world resulted in the great revelation of God's love. The highest glory of God's love was manifested in the self-sacrifice of Christ. It is the highest glory of the believer to be like his Lord. Without entire self-sacrifice, the new command of love cannot be fulfilled. Without entire self-sacrifice, we cannot love as Jesus loved. "Be ye followers of God," says the apostle, "and walk in love, as Christ hath loved us, and hath given himself for us." Let all your walk and conversation be, according to Christ's example, in love. It was this love that made His sacrifice acceptable in God's sight, a sweet-smelling savor. As His love exhibited itself in self-sacrifice, let your love prove itself to be conformable to His in the daily self-sacrifice for the welfare of others, so will it also be acceptable in the sight of God. "We ought to lay down our lives for the brethren."

Especially in the daily affairs of home life, in the relationship between husband and wife, in the relationship of employer and worker, Christ's self-sacrifice must be the rule of our walk. "Husbands, love your wives, even as Christ also loved the church, and *gave himself for it*" (Eph. 5:25).

Mark the words, "Hath given himself *for us* an offering *to God*." We see that self-sacrifice has two sides. Christ's self-sacrifice had a Godward as well as a manward aspect. It was *for us*, but it was *to God* that He offered himself as a sacrifice. In all our self-sacrifice there must be these two sides in union, though now the one and then again the other may be more prominent.

It is only when we sacrifice ourselves *to God* that there will be the power for an entire self-sacrifice. The Holy Spirit reveals to the believer the right of God's claim on us, how we are not our own but His. The realization of how absolutely we are God's property, bought and paid for with blood, of how we are loved with such a wonderful love, and of what blessedness there is in the full surrender to Him, leads the believer to yield himself as a whole burnt offering. He lays himself on the altar of consecration, and finds it his highest joy to be a sweet-smelling savor *to his God*, God-devoted and God-accepted. Then it becomes his most earnest desire to know how God would have him demonstrate this entire self-sacrifice in life and walk.

God points him to Christ's example. He was a sweet-smelling savor to God when He gave himself a sacrifice *for us*. For every believer who gives himself entirely to His service, God has the same honor as He had for His Son: He uses him as an instrument of blessing to others. Therefore John says, "He that loveth not his brother whom he hath seen, how can he love God whom he hath not seen?" (1 John 4:20). The self-sacrifice in which you have devoted yourself to God's service binds you also to serve your fellowmen; the same act which makes you entirely God's makes you entirely theirs.

It is this surrender to God that gives the power for self-sacrifice toward others, and even makes it a joy. When faith perceives the promise, "Inasmuch as ye have done it to the least of these my brethren, ye have done it unto me," I understand the glorious harmony between sacrifice *to God* and sacrifice *for men*. My relationship with my fellowmen, instead of being a hindrance to unbroken communion with God, becomes an opportunity of offering myself unceasingly to Him.

Blessed calling to walk in love as Christ loved us and gave himself for us a sacrifice and sweet-smelling savor to God! Only thus can the Church fulfill its destiny, and prove to the world that she is set apart to continue Christ's work of self-sacrificing love, and fill up that which remaineth behind of the afflictions of Christ.

But does God really expect us to deny ourselves so entirely for others? Is it not asking too much? Can anyone really sacrifice himself so entirely? Believer! God does expect it. Nothing less than this is the conformity to the image of His Son to which He predestinated you from eternity. This is the path by which Jesus entered into His glory and blessedness, and by no other path can the disciple enter into the joy of His Lord. *It is our calling to become exactly like Jesus in His love and self-sacrifice.* "Walk in love *as* Christ also loved."

It is marvelous when a believer sees and acknowledges this.

Ignorance of this is the number one cause for the impotence of the Church. In this matter the Church truly needs a second reformation. In the great Reformation, the power of Christ's atoning death and righteousness were brought to light, to the great comfort and joy of anxious souls. But we need a second reformation to lift the banner of Christ's example as our law, to restore the truth of the power of Christ's resurrection as it makes us partakers of the life and the likeness of our Lord. We must not only believe in the full union with our *surety* of reconciliation, but with our *head* as our *example* for life. We must represent Christ upon earth, and *let men see in the members* how the Head lived when He was in the flesh. Let us earnestly pray that believer's everywhere may be taught concerning their holy calling.

Do not fear to yield yourselves to God in the great act of a Christlike self-sacrifice! In conversion you gave yourself to God. In many acts of self-surrender since then you have again given yourselves to Him. But experience has taught you how much is still lacking. Perhaps you never knew how entire the self-sacrifice must be and could be. Come and see in Christ your example and in His sacrifice of himself on the cross *what your Father expects of you.* Come now and see in Christ—for He is your head and life—*what He will enable you to be and do.* Believe that what He accomplished on earth in His life and death as your example, He will now accomplish in you from heaven. Offer yourself to the Father in Christ, with the desire to be as entirely and completely as He, an offering and a sacrifice to God, *given up to God for men.* Expect Christ to work this in you and to maintain it. Let your relationship to God be clear and distinct: you, like Christ, wholly given up to Him. Then it will no longer be impossible to walk in love as Christ loved us. Then all your relationships with others will be the most glorious opportunity of proving before God how completely you have given yourself to *Him*—an offering and a sacrifice for a sweet-smelling savor.

O my God, who am I that you should choose me to be conformed to the image of your Son in His self-sacrificing love? In this is His divine perfection and glory, that He loved not His own life, but freely offered it for us to you in death. And in this I may be like Him; in a walk in love I may prove that I too have offered myself wholly to you.

O my Father, your purpose is mine; afresh I affirm my consecration to you. I cannot accomplish this in my own strength, but in the strength of Him who gave himself for me. Because Christ, my example, is also my life, I venture to say it: Father, in Christ, like Christ, I yield myself a sacrifice to you for men.

Father, teach me how to manifest your love to the world. You will do it by filling me with your love. Father, do it, that I may walk in love, *even as* Christ loved us. May I live every day as one who has the power of your Holy Spirit to enable me to love everyone with whom I come in contact, under every possible circumstance, to love with a love which is for you. Amen.

9

Not of the World

"These are in the world. . . . The world hath hated them, because they are not of the world, even as I am not of the world. . . . They are not of the world, even as I am not of the world" (John 17:11, 14, 16).

"As he is, so are we in this world" (1 John 4:17).

If Jesus was not of the world, why was He in the world? If there was no sympathy between Him and the world, why was it that He lived in it and did not remain in that high and holy world to which He belonged? The answer is: The Father had sent Him into the world. In these two expressions, "in the world," "not of the world," we find the whole secret of His work as Savior, of His glory as the God-man.

In the world—as a man because God would show that mankind belonged to Him, and not to the god of this world; that man was made to receive the divine life, and in this divine life to reach its highest glory.

In the world—in fellowship with men, to enter into loving relationship with them, to be seen and known of them, and thus to win them back to the Father.

In the world—in the struggle with the powers which rule the world, to learn obedience, and so to perfect and sanctify human nature.

Not of the world—but of heaven, to manifest and bring to

man the life that is in God, and which man had lost that men might see and desire it.

Not of the world—witnessing against its sin and departure from God, its impotence to know and please God.

Not of the world—founding a kingdom entirely heavenly in origin and nature, entirely independent of all that the world holds desirable or necessary, with principles and laws the very opposite of those that rule in the world.

Not of the world—in order to redeem all who trust in Him and to bring them into the new and heavenly kingdom which He had revealed.

In the world, not of the world. These two expressions reveal the great mystery of the person and work of the Savior. "Not *of* the world," in the power of His divine holiness judging and overcoming it; still *in* the world, and through His humanity and love seeking and saving all who desire to be saved. The most entire separation from the world, with the closest fellowship with those in the world—these two extremes meet in Jesus. In His own person He has reconciled them. And it is the calling of the believer to prove that these two dispositions, however much they may seem at variance, can be united in our life in perfect harmony. In each believer there must be seen a heavenly life shining out through earthly forms.

To take one of these two truths and exclusively cultivate it is not difficult. Some have taken "not of the world" as their motto. From the earliest ages until now these have thought they must escape to cloisters and deserts to serve God. They seek to show their devotion by severity in judging all this in the world and have counted this the only true religion. There was separation from sin, but there was also little or no fellowship with sinners. The sinner could not feel that he was surrounded with the atmosphere of a tender heavenly love. It was a one-sided and therefore a defective religion.

Then there are those who, on the other side, lay stress on "in the world," and appeal to the word of the apostle, "For then must ye needs go out of the world." They think that by showing that religion does not make us hermits or incapable of enjoying all there is to enjoy, they will induce the world to serve God.

They may succeed in making the world very religious, but the price is always too high—religion becomes very worldly.

The true follower of Jesus must combine both. If he does not demonstrate that he is not of the world, and exemplify a heavenly life, how will he convince the world of sin, or show that there is a higher life and thus create a desire for what the world does not yet possess? Commitment, holiness, and separation from the spirit of the world must characterize him. His heavenly spirit must manifest that he belongs to a kingdom not of this world. An unworldly, an other-worldly, a heavenly spirit must breathe in him.

And still he must live as one who is "in the world." Expressly placed here by God, among those who are of the world, to win their hearts, to acquire influence over them, and to communicate to them the life of the Spirit—this must be the great mission of his life. Not as the wisdom of the world would teach, by yielding, and complying, and softening the calling to discipleship, will he succeed. No, but only by walking in the footsteps of Him who alone can teach how to be in the world and yet not of it. He can be a blessing to the world only by a life of serving and suffering love, in which the believer distinctly confesses that the glory of God is the aim of his existence, and in which, full of the Holy Spirit, he brings men into direct contact with the love of God.

Oh, who will teach us the secret of uniting in our lives what seems so difficult—to be in the world and not of the world? He can do it who has said: "They are not of the world, *even as* I am not of the world." That *"even as"* has a deeper meaning and power than we know. If we allow the Holy Spirit to unfold that word to us, we will understand what it is to be in the world as He was in the world. That *"even as"* has its root and strength in a life union. In it we discover the divine secret, that *the more entirely one is not of the world, the more capable he is to be in the world*. The more freedom one has from the spirit and principles of the world, the more influence he will exert in it.

The life of the world is self-pleasing and self-exaltation. The life of heaven is holy, self-denying love. The weakness of many believers who seek to separate themselves from the world is that they have too much of the spirit of the world. Even in separation they seek their own happiness and perfection. Jesus Christ was not of the world and had nothing of its spirit; this is why He could love sinners, could win them and save them. The believer is to be the same. The Lord says: "Not of the world, even as I am not of the world." Through the new birth he has the life and love of heaven in him; this supernatural, heavenly life gives him power to be in the world without being of it. The disciple who believes fully in the Christlikeness of his inner life will experience the truth of it. He cultivates and gives utterance to the assurance: "Even as Christ, so am I not of the world, because I am in Christ." He understands that only in close union with Christ can his separation from the world be maintained; to the extent that Christ lives in him can he lead a heavenly life. The only answer to his calling is, on the one side, as crucified to the world to withdraw himself from its power; and, on the other, as living in Christ to go into it and bless it. He lives in heaven and walks on earth.

Can you see the true imitation of Jesus Christ? "Wherefore come out from among them, and be ye separate, saith the Lord." Then the promise is fulfilled, "I will dwell in them and walk in them." Then Christ sends you, as the Father sent Him, to be in the world as the place ordained of your Father to glorify Him and to make known His love. It is not so much in the desire to leave earth for heaven as in the willingness to live the life of heaven here on earth that the believer manifests the life of God.

"Not of the world" is not only a separation from the world, but is the living manifestation of the spirit, and the love, and the power of heaven.

O Thou great High Priest! You have prayed for us to the Father, as those who do not belong to the world, and still must remain in it. May your all-prevailing intercession now be effectual in our behalf.

The world still has entrance to our hearts, its selfish spirit is still too much within us. Through unbelief the new life has not always its full power. Lord, we beseech you, as the fruit of your all-powerful intercession, let that word be fully realized in us: "Not of the world, even as I am not of the world." Our likeness to you is our only power against the world.

Lord, we can be like you only when we are one with you. We can walk like you only when we abide in you. Blessed Lord, we surrender ourselves to abide in you alone. You have promised to take entire possession of a life entirely given to you. Let your Holy Spirit, who dwells in us, unite us so closely with yourself that we may always live as not of the world. And let your Spirit so make known to us your work in the world that it may be our joy in deep humility and fervent love to demonstrate to all what a blessed life there is in the world for those who are not of the world. May the proof that we are not of the world be the tenderness and fervency with which, like you, we sacrifice ourselves for those who are in the world. Amen.

10

In His Heavenly Mission

"As thou hast sent me into the world, even so have I also sent them into the world" (John 17:18).
"As my Father hath sent me, even so send I you" (John 20:21).

The Lord Jesus lived here on earth under a deep conscious-ness of having a mission from His Father to fulfill. He contin-ually used the expression, "The Father hath sent me."[1] He knew what this mission was. He knew the Father had chosen Him, and sent Him into the world with the one purpose of fulfilling that mission, and He knew the Father would give Him all that He needed for it. Faith in the Father having sent Him was the motive and power for all that He did.

Among the nations it is a great help if an ambassador knows clearly what his mission is; that he has nothing to do but to care for its accomplishment; and that he has given himself un-dividedly to do this one thing. For the believer it is of no less consequence that he should know that he has a mission, what its nature is, and how he is to accomplish it.

---

[1]It will repay the trouble to compare carefully the following passages: John 5:24, 30, 37, 38; 6:38, 39, 40, 44; 7:16, 28, 29, 33; 8:16, 18, 26, 29, 42; 9:4; 11:42; 12:44, 45, 49; 13:20; 14:24; 15:21; 16:28; 17:8, 18, 21, 23, 25; 20:21. Christ wanted men to know that He did not act independently, but on behalf of An-other who had sent Him. The consciousness of a mission never left Him for a moment.

Our heavenly mission is one of the most glorious parts of our conformity to Christ. He states it plainly in the most solemn moments of His life: "As my Father hath sent me," so send I my disciples. In His high-priestly prayer this is the ground upon which He asks for their keeping and sanctification. He says it to the disciples after His resurrection, as the ground on which they are to receive the Holy Spirit. Nothing will help us more to know and fulfill our mission than to realize how perfectly it corresponds to the mission of Christ; how they are, in fact, identical.

Our mission is like His *in its object*. Why did the Father send His Son? To make known His love and His will in redeeming sinners. He was to do this, not only by word and precept, but in His own person, disposition, and conduct, exhibiting the Father's holy love. He was to so represent the unseen Father in heaven that men on earth might know what the Father was like.

After the Lord had fulfilled His mission, He ascended into heaven and became to the world like the Father, the unseen One. He has committed His mission to His disciples after showing them how to fulfill it. They must so represent Him that from seeing them, men can judge what He is like. Every believer should so mirror the image of Jesus—so exhibit in his person and conduct the same love to sinners as animated Christ—that from them the world may know what Christ is like. Oh, my soul! take time to realize these heavenly thoughts: Our mission is like Christ's in its object: demonstrating the holy love of heaven in earthly form.

Like Christ's *in its origin, too*. It was the Father's love that chose Christ for this work, and counted Him worthy of such honor and trust. We also are chosen by Christ for this work. Every believer knows that it was not that he sought the Lord, but that the Lord sought and chose him. In that seeking and drawing the Lord had expressed this heavenly mission: "You have not chosen me, but I have chosen you and ordained you, that you should go and bring forth fruit."

Remember that the Lord, who knows you and your place in life, has need of you and has chosen you to be His representative in the circle in which you move. Fix your heart on this. He has fixed His heart on you that you might demonstrate to those around you the very image of His unseen glory. Oh, think of the origin of your heavenly mission in His everlasting love, as His had its origin in the love of the Father. Your mission is in very truth just like His.

Like it, too, *in the equipping for it.* Every ambassador expects to be supplied with all that he needs for his embassy. "He who hath sent me is with me. The Father hath not left me alone." That word tells us how the Father was always with the Son, the source of strength and comfort. Even so the Church of Christ in her mission: "Go ye and teach all nations" has the promise: "Lo, I am with you alway." The believer need never hold back because of deficiency. The Lord does not demand anything which He does not give the power to perform. Every believer may depend on it, that as the Father gave His Holy Spirit to the Son to equip Him for His work, so the Lord Jesus will give His people all they need. The grace to demonstrate Christ, to exhibit the lovely light of His example and likeness, and like Christ himself to be a fountain of love and life and blessing to all around, is given to everyone who only heartily and believingly takes up his heavenly calling. The sender cares for all that is needful for the sent ones.

And like also *in the consecration which it demands.* The Lord Jesus gave himself entirely and undividedly to accomplish His work. He lived for it alone. "I must work the works of him that sent me, while it is day: the night cometh, when no man can work." The Father's mission was the only reason of His being on earth; for that alone He would live: to reveal to mankind what a glorious God the Father in heaven is.

As with Jesus, so with us. Christ's mission is *the only reason for our being on earth*; were it not for that, He would take us away. Most believers do not believe this. Fulfilling Christ's mission is for them something to be done along with many other things, for which it is difficult to find time and strength. And yet it is so certainly true: to accomplish Christ's mission is the only reason for my being upon earth. When I believe this, and like my Lord consecrate myself undividedly to it, I indeed live well-pleasing to Him. This heavenly mission is so great and glorious that without an entire consecration to it we cannot accomplish it. Without this, the powers which equip us cannot take possession of us. Without this, we have no liberty to expect the Lord's wonderful help and the fulfillment of all His blessed promises. *Just as with Jesus, our heavenly mission demands nothing less than entire consecration.* Am I prepared for this? Then I have indeed the key through which the holy glories of this word of Jesus will be revealed to my experience: "As my Father hath sent me, even so send I you."

Oh, brethren, this heavenly mission is indeed worthy that we devote ourselves entirely to it as the only thing we live for!

Lord Jesus, you descended from heaven to show us what the life of heaven is. You could do this because you were of heaven. You brought the image and Spirit of the heavenly life to earth. And with it you did so gloriously exhibit what constitutes the very glory of heaven: the will and love of the unseen Father.

Lord, you are now the invisible One in heaven, and have sent us to represent you in your heavenly glory as Savior! You said that we should so love men that from us they may form some idea of how you love them in heaven.

Blessed Lord, my heart cries out: How can you send me with such a calling? How can you expect it when I have so little love? How can I demonstrate the life of heaven?

Precious Savior, my soul blesses you that you do not demand more than you give. You who are the life of heaven, you live in your disciples. Blessed be your holy name, I have your Holy Spirit as my life breath. He is the heavenly life of my soul: I surrender to the leading of the Spirit to fulfill Christ's mission. In the joy and power of the Holy Spirit I can be your image-bearer, can show to men in some measure what your likeness is.

Lord, teach me and all your people to understand that we are not of the world as you were not of the world, and therefore are sent by you even as you were sent of the Father: to prove in our life that we are of that world, full of love, and purity, and blessing. Amen.

11

As the Elect of God

*"He also did predestinate to be conformed to the image of his
Son, that he might be the firstborn among many brethren"* (Rom.
8:29).

Scripture teaches us a personal election. It does this not only
in isolated verses; it runs throughout the Bible. The working
out of the counsels of eternity into history proves it. We see
continually how much of the future of God's kingdom can depend upon the faithful service of a single person. In carrying
out God's purpose, His foreordaining of individuals is instru-
mental. The history of the world and of God's kingdom, as of
the individual believer, has its sure foundation upon God's
counsels from eternity.

There have always been divergent views on predestination
among believers. Some are so afraid of interfering with human
responsibility that they totally reject any predestinating work
on God's part. Scripture does not share this fear. Nor does it
share the fear of those who so stress God's predestinating work
as to eliminate all human responsibility. It teaches us that there
is place for both of these truths, though we may differ as to the
extent we emphasize either. No doubt in eternity the role of
both will be clarified. For now it is important that we grasp
both in faith and allow God to teach us where they seem in
conflict. The stronger your faith in God's everlasting purpose,

the more your courage will be strengthened for work; on the other hand, the more you work and are blessed, the clearer you will understand the purposes of God.

For this reason it is of so much consequence for a believer to make his election sure (2 Pet. 1:10). The Scriptures assure that if we do this, "we shall never fall." The more I see how this election has reference to every part of my calling, the more I will be strengthened in the conviction that God himself will perfect His work in me, and that it is possible for me to be all He expects. With every duty Scripture lays upon me, with every promise for whose fulfillment I desire, I will find in God's purposes the firm footing upon which my expectations may rest, and the true measure by which they are to be guided. I shall understand that my life on earth is meant in God's purposes to be a copy of the heavenly life the Father has drawn out in Christ. Therefore, make your calling and election sure; let it become clear to you that in Christ you are elected and that there is a goal: "If ye do these things, ye shall never fall." Quiet communion with God on the basis of His unchangeable purpose imparts an immovable firmness that keeps us from stumbling.

One of the most blessed expressions in regard to God's purpose concerning us in Christ is this word: "For whom he did foreknow, he also did predestinate to be conformed to the image of his Son." *Christ Jesus is the elect of God; in Him election has its beginning and ending.* "In him we are chosen"; it is only in our union with Him and for His glory that our election is seen. The believer who seeks in election merely the certainty of his own salvation, or relief from fear and doubt, knows very little of its real glory. The purposes of election embrace all the riches that are prepared for us in Christ, and reach to every moment and every need of our lives. "Chosen . . . in him . . . that we should be holy and without blame before him in love" (Eph. 1:4). We may differ on the means, but surely we must agree that holiness is the goal. Only when the connection between election and sanctification is rightly understood in the Church will the doctrine of election bring its full blessing (2 Thess. 2:13; 1 Pet. 1:2). It teaches the believer how God will work in him, and how he may rely even in the smallest matters upon the unchangeable purpose of God to work out itself in the accomplishment of everything that He expects of His people. In this light the word "predestinated to be conformed to the image of his Son" gives new strength to everyone who has begun to take *what Christ is* as the rule of *what he himself is to be.*

If your desire is to be *like Christ,* fix your mind on how clearly this is God's will concerning you; how the whole of redemption has been planned with the view of your becoming so; how God's purpose is the guarantee that your desires will be fulfilled. All the divine powers which have already accomplished the first part of the eternal purpose—the revealing of the Father's perfect likeness in the man Christ Jesus—are equally engaged to accomplish the second part and to work that likeness in each of His children. In the work of Christ there is perfect provision for the carrying out of God's purposes. Our union to Christ, held fast in a living faith, will be an all-prevailing power. Joined to Christ we can depend upon His eternal purposes to be accomplished with divine certainty if we continue to yield ourselves to it. Is this not God's purpose to conform us to the image of His Son?

The living consciousness of this truth will have a powerful impact on us. It teaches us to yield ourselves to the Father who has demonstrated in Christ the divine power to effect His purpose in us. It shows us how impotent our own efforts are to accomplish this work. God's purposes are totally joined to Jesus Christ. He who is the beginning must be the middle and the end. In a very wonderful manner it strengthens our faith with a holy boldness to glory in God alone, and to expect from God the fulfillment of every promise and every command, of every part of the purpose of His blessed will.

What is this likeness to Christ? *It is sonship.* It is to the image of *His Son* we are to be conformed. All the traits of a Christlike life resolve themselves into this one as their spring and end. We are "predestinated . . . unto the adoption of *children* by Jesus Christ" (Eph. 1:5). It was *as the Son* Christ lived and served and pleased the Father. It is only *as a son* with the spirit of His own *Son* in my heart that I can live and serve and please the Father. I must daily walk in the full and clear consciousness: like Christ, I am a son of the Most High God, born from above, the beloved of the Father. As a son the Father is actively providing for my every need. As a son I live in dependence and trust, in love and obedience, in joy and hope. It is when I live with the Father as a son that it becomes possible to make any sacrifice and to obey every command.

Believer! take time to pray over this truth until it exercises its full power in your soul. Let the Holy Spirit write it into your inmost being, that God's eternal purpose is to conform you to the image of His Son. The Father's object was the honor of His Son, "that he might be the first-born among many brethren." Let this be your object too in all your life, so to demonstrate the image of your elder brother that others may be pointed to Him alone, may praise Him alone, and seek to follow Him more closely. Let it be the fixed and only purpose of your life, the great object of your believing prayer, that "Christ be magnified in my body." This will give you new confidence to ask and expect all that is necessary to live like Christ.

Your conformity to Christ will be one of the links connecting the eternal purpose of the Father with the eternal fulfillment of it in glorifying the Son. Your conformity to Christ becomes such a holy, heavenly, divine work that you realize it can come only from the Father, and that from Him you can and shall receive it. What God's purpose has decreed, God's power will perform. What God's love has ordained and commanded, God's love will most certainly accomplish. A living faith in His eternal purpose will become one of the mightiest powers in urging and helping us to live *like Christ*.

Eternal Father, I bow before you in the deepest humility. It has been such a strength to discover that in union with your Son, I too am chosen, in order to send me into the world as you sent Him. You have shown me that this mission to be as He was in the world was your decree from eternity. O my God, my soul bows prostrate in the dust before you.

Lord God, now that in your Son I see the fulfillment of your own purpose, I dare confidently look for an answer. Your will is stronger than any hindrance. The faith that trusts you will not be put to shame. Lord, in holy reverence and worship, and with childlike confidence and hope, I utter this prayer: Father, give me the desire of my soul, conformity to the image of your Son; Father, likeness to Jesus, this is what my soul desires. Let me, like Him, be your holy child.

O my Father, write it in your book of remembrance, and write it in my remembrance too, that I have asked you for what I desire above all things, conformity to the image of your Son.

Father, to this you have destined me. You will give it to me for your glory. Amen.

12

In Doing God's Will

"For I came down from heaven not to do my own will, but the will of him that sent me" (John 6:38; 5:30).

In the will of God we have the highest expression of His divine perfection, and at the same time the high-energy of His divine power. Creation owes its being and its beauty to it; it is the manifestation of God's will. In heaven the angels find their highest blessedness in doing God's will. For this man was created with a free will in order that he might have the power to choose of his own accord to do God's will. But man committed the great sin of doing his own rather than God's will. *Yes, his own rather than God's will!* That is the root and the wretchedness of sin.

Jesus Christ became man to bring us back to the blessedness of *doing God's will.* The great object of redemption was to make us and our will free from the power of sin, and to lead us again to live and do the will of God. In His life on earth Christ showed us what it is to live only for the will of God. In His death and resurrection He won for us the power to live and do the will of God as He had done.

"Lo, I come to do thy will, O God." These words, uttered through the Holy Spirit by the mouth of one of His prophets long ages before Christ's birth, are the key to His life on earth. At Nazareth in the carpenter's shop, at the Jordan with John the Baptist, in the wilderness with Satan, in public with the multitude, in living and dying, it was this that inspired and guided and gladdened Him: the glorious will of the Father was to be accomplished in Him and by Him.

Let us not underestimate what this cost Him. He says repeatedly, "*Not my will*, but the will of the Father," to show us that there was in very deed a denial of His own will. In Gethsemane the sacrifice of His own will reached its height, but what took place there was only the perfect expression of what had rendered His whole life acceptable to the Father. Sin is not seen necessarily when a person's will is different from the Creator's, but in this, that he clings to his own will when it is seen to be contrary to the will of the Creator. As man, Jesus had a human will. As man, He did not always know beforehand what the will of God was. He had to wait, and be taught of God, and learn from time to time what that will was. But when the will of His Father was once known to Him, then He was always ready to give up His own human will and do the will of the Father. It was this that constituted the perfection and the value of His self-sacrifice. He had once for all surrendered himself as a man, to live only in and for the will of God, and was always ready, even to the sacrifice of Gethsemane and Calvary, to do that will alone.

It is *this life of obedience*, accomplished by the Lord Jesus in the flesh, that is not only imputed to us but *imparted through the Holy Spirit*. Through His death our Lord Jesus has atoned for our self-will and disobedience. It was by conquering it in His own perfect obedience that He atoned for it. He has not only blotted out the guilt of our self-will before God but broken its power in us. In His resurrection He brought from the dead a life that had conquered and destroyed all self-will. And the believer who knows the power of Jesus' death and resurrection has the power to consecrate himself entirely to God's will. He knows that the call to follow Christ means nothing less than to embrace the words of the Master: "I seek not my own will, but the will of the Father."

Here we must begin by taking the same stand that our Lord did. Take God's will as the only thing for which you live on earth. Look at the sun and moon, the grass and flowers, and see that each of them has its glory only because it is doing God's will. But they do it without knowing it. We do it still more gloriously because we know and will to do it. Let your heart be filled with the thought of the glory of God's will concerning His children, and concerning you and declare that it is your one purpose to do His will. Yield yourself to the Father frequently and distinctly, acknowledging that it is a settled matter that His beautiful and blessed will must and shall be done. Say it frequently in quiet meditation with a joyful and trusting heart: "Praise God! I may live only to do the will of God."

Let no fear keep you back from this. Do not think that this will be too hard to do. God's will seems hard only when viewed from a distance and when refusing to submit to it. Look again how beautiful the will of God makes everything in nature. Ask yourself, Is it right to distrust Him who loves you as His child? The will of God is the will of His love. How can you fear to surrender yourself to it?

Never allow the fear of not being able to obey that will to keep you back. The Son of God came on earth to show what the life of man may become. His resurrection life gives us power to live as He lived. Jesus Christ enables us, through His Spirit, to walk not after the flesh but according to the will of God.

"I come to do thy will, O God." Even a believer in the Old Testament was able, through the Spirit, to speak that word for himself as well as for Christ. Christ took it up and filled it with new life-power. And now He expects that believers will even more heartily and entirely make it their choice. Let us do so. We must not first try and see whether we occasionally succeed in doing God's will. No, this is not the right way. Let us first recognize God's will as a whole, and the claims it has upon us, as well as its blessedness and glory. Let us surrender ourselves to it as to God himself, and consider it as one of the first articles of our creed: I am in the world, like Christ, only to do the Father's will. This surrender will teach us to joyfully accept every command and every providence as part of the will we have already yielded ourselves to. This surrender will give us courage to wait for God's sure guidance and strength, because the man who lives only for God's will may depend upon God's provision. This surrender will not only deepen the consciousness of our utter impotence but will also deepen the fellowship and the likeness of the beloved Son, and make us partakers of all the blessedness and love that the Son has prepared for us. There is nothing that will bring us closer to God in union to Christ than loving and doing the will of God.

Child of God! one of the first marks of conformity to Christ is obedience—simple and implicit obedience to all the will of God. Let it be the most marked thing in your life. Begin by willingly and wholeheartedly keeping every known scriptural command of God. Go on to a very tender yielding to everything that conscience tells you to be right, even when the Word does not directly command it. So shall you rise higher; obedience to the known commandments and to conscience wherever it speaks are the preparation for a deeper teaching into the meaning and application of the Word, and into a more direct and spiritual insight into God's will. It is to those *who obey* Him that God gives the Holy Spirit, through whom the blessed will of God becomes the light that shines ever more brightly on our path. "If any man *will do his will*, he shall know." Blessed will of God! blessed obedience to God's will!—oh, that we knew to count and keep these as our most precious treasures!

And should it appear too hard to live only for God's will, let us remember where Christ found His strength: it was because it was the Father's *will* that the Son rejoiced to do it. "This commandment have I received *of my Father*." This made even the sacrifice of His life possible. Our union to Jesus and our calling to live like Him ever point us to *His sonship* as the secret of His life and strength. Let us build into our lives this thought: I am the Father's beloved child; each commandment is an expression of the Father's *will*; a Christlike sense of sonship leads to a Christlike obedience.

O my God, thank you for the wondrous gift that your Son became a man and taught us how we may do your will. Thank you for the glorious calling to be like Him in this too, with Him to taste the blessedness of a life in perfect harmony with your glorious and perfect will. Thank you that in this too I may be like the first-begotten Son.

I come now, O my Father, to take up my calling in childlike, joyous trust and love. Lord, I would live wholly and only to do your will. I would abide in the Word and wait upon the Spirit. I want, like your Son, to live in fellowship with you in prayer, in the firm confidence that you will cause me to know your will more clearly. O my Father, let this desire be acceptable in your sight. Keep it in the thoughts of my heart forever. Give me grace with true joy to continually say: Not my will, but the will of my Father must be done. I am here on earth only to do the will of my God. Amen.

13

In His Compassion

"Then Jesus . . . said, I have compassion on the multitude" (Matt. 15:32).

"Shouldest not thou also have had compassion on thy fellow-servant, even as I had pity on thee?" (Matt. 18:32).

On three different occasions Matthew tells us that our Lord was moved with compassion on the multitude. His whole life was a manifestation of the compassion with which He had looked on every sinner that ever lived, and of the tenderness with which He was moved at the sight of misery and sorrow. He was the true reflection of our compassionate God—like the father who, moved with compassion toward his prodigal son, fell on his neck and kissed him.

In this compassion, we see that Jesus did not look upon the will of God as a duty or an obligation, but that the divine will was dwelling within Him as His own, inspiring and ruling all His feelings and motives. After He had said, "I came down from heaven not to do mine own will, but the will of him that sent me," He added, "And this is the Father's will . . . that of all which he hath given me I should lose nothing, but should raise it up again at the last day. And this is the will of him that sent me, that every one which . . . believeth on him, may have everlasting life" (John 6:37–39). For Jesus, the will of God did not consist in certain things which were forbidden or commanded.

73

No. He had entered into that which forms the very heart of God's will, that to lost sinners He should give eternal life. Because God himself is love, His will is that love should have full scope in the salvation of sinners. The Lord Jesus came down to earth in order to manifest and accomplish this will of God. He did not do this as a servant obeying the will of a stranger. In His personal life and attitudes, He proved that the loving will of His Father to save sinners was His own. Not only His death on Golgotha, but just as much the compassion in which He took and bore the need of all the wretched, and the tenderness of His relationship with them, was proof that the Father's will had truly become His own. In every way He demonstrated that life is only meaningful when it is viewed as the opportunity of doing the will of His Father.

Followers of Christ must allow the will of the Father to be to them what it was to their Lord. The will of the Father in the mission of His Son was the manifestation and the triumph of divine compassion in the salvation of lost sinners. Jesus could not possibly accomplish this will in any other way than by having and showing this compassion. *God's will for us is what it was for Jesus: the salvation of the perishing.* It is impossible for us to fulfill that will other than by demonstrating in our lives the compassion of our God. The seeking of God's will must not be only denying ourselves that which God forbids and doing that which God commands, but must include the surrender of ourselves to have the same mind and attitude toward sinners that God has. By our personal devotion to every perishing sinner around us, and by our helping them in compassionate love, we demonstrate that the will of God has become our will. With the compassionate God as our Father, with Christ who was so often moved with compassion as our life, nothing can be more natural than the command that the believer's life should be one of compassionate love.

Compassion is the spirit of love which is awakened by the sight of need or wretchedness. Each day gives abundant occasion for the practice of this heavenly virtue in a world so full of misery and sin! Every believer should by prayer and practice cultivate a compassionate heart, as one of the most precious marks of likeness to the blessed Master. Everlasting love longs to give itself to a perishing world, and to find its satisfaction in saving the lost. *It seeks for vessels which it may fill with the love of God, and send out among the dying that they may drink and live forever.* It seeks hearts that will consider it their highest privilege, as the dispensers of God's compassion, to live entirely to bless and save sinners. The everlasting compassion which has had mercy on you calls you to come and let it fill you. Compassion will equip you to be a witness to God's compassionate love.

The opportunity for showing compassion is all around us. There are the poor and the sick, widows and orphans, distressed and depressed souls, who need nothing so much as the refreshment a compassionate heart can bring. They live in the midst of believers and yet sometimes complain that sinners have more sympathy than those saints. Believers, pray earnestly for a compassionate heart, always on the lookout for an opportunity of doing some work of love, always ready to be an instrument of the divine compassion. It was the compassion of Jesus that attracted so many to Him; that same compassionate tenderness will still, more than anything, draw souls to you and to your Lord.[1]

And how much of spiritual misery surrounds us on all sides! Here is an empty rich man. There is a foolish, thoughtless youth. There is a poor drunkard or a hopeless unfortunate. Or perhaps simply people entirely caught up in the follies of the world which surround them. How often are words of unloving indifference, or harsh judgment, or slothful hopelessness heard concerning these! The compassionate heart is lacking. Compassion looks upon the deepest misery as the place prepared for her by God, and is attracted by it. Compassion never wearies, never gives up hope. Compassion will now allow itself to be rejected, for it is the self-denying love of Christ which inspires it.

The Christian does not confine his compassion to his own circle; he has a large heart. His Lord has declared the whole heathen world as his field of labor. He seeks to be acquainted

---

[1]See the note at the end of the chapter.

with the circumstances of the heathen: he carries their burden on his heart; he is really moved with compassion, and means to help them. Whether near or far off, whether he witnesses it in all its filth and degradation, or only hears of it, compassionate love lives only to accomplish God's will in saving the perishing.

Like Christ in His compassion: let this be our motto. After uttering the parable of the Samaritan who, "moved with compassion," helped the wounded stranger, the Lord said, "Go and do likewise." He is himself the compassionate Samaritan, who speaks to every believer, "Go and do likewise." *Even as* I have done to you, do you likewise. We who owe everything to His compassion, who profess ourselves His followers, who walk in His footsteps and bear His image, oh, Let us exhibit His compassion to the world. We can do it. He lives in us; His Spirit works in us. Let us with much prayer and firm faith look to *His example as the sure promise of what we can be.* It will be to Him an unspeakable joy if He finds us prepared for it, not only to show His compassion to us, but through us to the world. And ours will be the unutterable joy of having a Christlike heart, full of compassion and great mercy.

O my Lord, my calling is becoming almost too high. In your compassionate love, I must follow and reproduce your life. It is the compassion with which I help bodily and spiritual misery, in the gentle, tender love which every sinner feels from me, that the world forms its idea of your compassion. Most merciful One! forgive me that the world has seen so little of it in me. Most mighty Redeemer! let your compassion not only save me, but so take hold of me and dwell in me that compassion may be the very breath and joy of my life. May your compassion toward me be within me a living fountain of compassion toward others.

Lord Jesus, I know you give this only on one condition, that I let go of my own life and my efforts to sanctify that life, and allow you to live in me as my life. Most merciful One, I yield myself to you! You alone have a right to me. There is nothing more precious to me than to be like you!

Lord, here I am. I have faith that you will teach and enable me to obey your word: "Thou shouldest have had compassion even as I had compassion on thee." In that faith I go out this very day to find in my relationships with others the opportunity of showing how you have loved me. In that faith it will become the great object of my life to win men to you. Amen.

NOTE

"Evil can be overcome only by the contact of a most personal self-devotion, never by a love that stands at a distance. 'Ye are the salt of the earth,' Jesus said; *ye yourselves* just as you are, in the midst of society; in every place and every moment a sanctifying power must flow out from you and your presence. Christ *himself* is the life and the light. In all that He does, or says, or suffers, it is always *himself*; whoever separates ought from himself no longer preserves it, it vanishes in his hands. And just this is the radical error of our modern Christianity. Men separate the words and works of Christ from himself, and so it comes that many, with all they do as Christians, have never found Christ himself. So there are many who trust in His suffering and merit, who cannot show that they have any real fellowship with Him, or truly follow Him. Christ had His abode not only in Cana of Galilee, but also in Gethsemane and on Calvary. Alas! are there not many who make their boast of the cross, and yet are more afraid of the real cross than they are of the devil? They have so wisely arranged their profession of Christ's cross that no loss to their honor, their goods, or their liberty can ever come from it. Christ's true and actual imitation must once again, as in the olden times, become the standard of Christendom. Only and alone in this way will faith again conquer unbelief and superstition. Many are laboring hard at present to prove to a doubting world the inspiration of Holy Scripture, the truth of the words and the life of the Lord Jesus. It is labor in vain to try to prove by words and argument that which can alone *be made known by its own self-evidencing power and its actual presence*! Let the proof be given in your deed, that the spirit of the miracles dwells in you; *prove above all in your life that Jesus Christ is continuing in you His heavenly eternal life;* and your words will bring many to believe. But if you are wanting in this demonstration of the Spirit and of power, be not surprised if the world bestow little attention on your eloquent arguments. The hour is come that all Christendom must rise up as one man, and *in the power of Christ repeat over again what Christ himself did to a perishing world.* This is the need, the imitation of Jesus Christ; this is the only valid proof for the truth of Christianity."[2]

---

[2]From M. Diemer, *Een nieuw boek van de navolging van Jesus Christus.*

14

In His Oneness with the Father

"Holy Father, keep through thine own name those whom thou hast given me, that they may be one, as we are. That they all may be one; as thou, Father, art in me, and I in thee, that they also may be one in us: that the world may believe that thou hast sent me. And the glory which thou gavest me I have given them; that they may be one, even as we are one: I in them, and thou in me, that they may be made perfect in one; and that the world may know that thou hast sent me, and hast loved them, as thou hast loved me" (John 17:11, 21, 22).

What an unspeakable treasure we have in this high-priestly prayer! There the heart of Jesus is laid open to our view, and we see what His love desires for us. There the heavens are opened to us, and we learn what He as our intercessor is continually asking and obtaining for us from the Father.

In that prayer the mutual union of believers occupies the largest place. In His prayer for all who in the future shall believe, this is the chief petition (vv. 20–26). Three times He repeats this prayer for their unity.

The Lord tells us plainly why He desires it so strongly. *This unity is the only convincing proof to the world that the Father had sent Him.* Despite its blindness, the world knows that selfishness is the curse of sin. It is of little influence when believers tell them that they are born again, that they are happy, that they can do wonders in Jesus' name, or can prove the reliability of the Scriptures. But when the world sees a church from which selfishness is banished, then it will acknowledge the divine mission of Christ who alone could work such a wonder, a community of believers who truly and heartily love one another.

The Lord speaks of this unity three times as the reflection of His own oneness with the Father. He knew that this was the perfection of the Godhead: the Father and Son as persons separate and yet perfectly one in the living fellowship of the Holy Spirit. And He cannot imagine anything higher than this, that believers should with Him and in Him be one with each other, even as He and the Father are one.

The intercession of the Lord Jesus avails much; it is all-prevailing. What He asks He receives of His Father. Unfortunately, the blessing which descends finds no entrance in hearts where there is no place prepared to receive it. How many believers desire to be one even as the Father and the Son are one? They are so accustomed to a life of selfishness and imperfect love that they do not even desire such perfect love: they put off that union until they meet in heaven. And yet the Lord was thinking of our life on earth when He twice said, "That the world may know."

That "they may be one, *even as* we are one." The Church must be awakened to understand and to value this prayer. This union is one of life and love at once. Some explain it as having reference to the hidden life-union which binds all believers together despite external divisions. But this is not what the Lord means; He speaks of something that the world can see, something that resembles the union between God the Father and God the Son. The hidden unity of life must be manifest in the visible unity and fellowship of love. Most believers consider it impossible to live in the full oneness of love with the children of God around them. Only when they learn that a life in love to each other is their simple duty, and begin to cry to God for His Holy Spirit to work it in them, will there be a hope of change in this respect. The fire will spread from circle to circle and from church to church until all who truly do the will of God will consecrate themselves to abide in love even as God is love.

And what are we to do now? Let everyone who believes the word of the Master, *"even as* I, so also ye," let him begin with his own circle. And in that circle with himself first. However weak or unlovely or trying the members of Christ's body may be with whom he is surrounded, let him live with them in close fellowship and love. Whether they are willing for it or not, whether they accept or reject it, let him love them with a Christ-like love. Yes, to love them as Christ does must be the purpose of his life. This love will find an echo in some hearts at least, and awaken in them the desire, too, to seek after the life of love and perfect oneness.

Such effort will also bring the discovery of the impotence of the believer to reach this standard! He will soon find that nothing will avail but a personal undivided consecration. To have a love like Christ's, I must truly have a life like Christ's: *I must live with His life.* The lesson must be learned anew, that Christ in the fullest sense of the word will be the life of those who dare to trust Him for it. Those who cannot trust with a full trust cannot love with a full love.

Believer, listen once more to the simple way to such a life. First acknowledge your calling to live and love like Christ. Confess your inability to fulfill this calling, even in the very least. Listen to the word, that Christ is waiting to enable you to fulfill this calling if you will give yourself unreservedly to Him. Make the surrender in this, that conscious of being utterly unable to do anything in your own strength, you offer yourself to the Lord to work in you both to will and to do. And then depend upon Him, who in the power of His unceasing intercession can save completely, to work in you what He has asked of His Father for you. Yes, count on Him who has said to the Father, "Thou in me and I in them, that they may be one, even as we are one," that He will manifest His life in you with heavenly power. As you live with His life, you will love with His love.

Beloved believers, the oneness of Christ with the Father is our model: even as they so must we be one. Let us love one another, serve one another, bear with one another, help one another, live for one another. For this our love is too small: but we will earnestly pray that Christ gives us His love wherewith to love. With God's love shed abroad in our hearts through the Holy Spirit, we shall be so one that the world will know that it is indeed the truth, that the Father sent Christ into the world and that Christ has given us the very life and love of heaven.

Holy Father, I know now with what petitions He, who ever lives to make intercession, continually approaches you. It is for the perfect unity of His disciples. Father, I too would cry for this blessing. Alas, how divided is your Church! It is not the division of language or country that is to be deplored, not even the difference of doctrine or teaching that is so grievous. But, Lord! it is the lack of unity of spirit and love whereby your Church should convince the world that she is from heaven.

O Lord, I confess before you with deep shame the coldness, and selfishness, and distrust, and bitterness that is still at times to be seen among your children. I confess before you my own lack of that fervent and perfect love to which you have called me. O forgive, and have mercy upon me.

Lord God, visit your people! It is through the one Spirit that we can know and show our unity in the one Lord. Let your Holy Spirit work powerfully in your believing people to make them one. Let it be felt in every circle where God's children meet each other, how indispensable a close union in the love of Jesus is. And let my heart, too, be delivered from self, to realize, in the fellowship with your children, how we are one, even as you and your Son are one. Amen.

15

In His Dependence on the Father

"Verily, verily, I say unto you, The Son can do nothing of himself, but what he seeth the Father do: for what things soever he doeth, these also doeth the Son likewise. For the Father loveth the Son, and showeth him all things that himself doeth: and he will show him greater works than these that ye may marvel" (John 5:19, 20).

"I know my own, and my own know me, as the Father knows me and I know the Father" (John 10:15, RSV).

Our relationship to Jesus is meant to be the exact counterpart of His to the Father. Thus, the words in which He sets forth His relationship with the Father have their truth in us too. The words of Jesus in John 5 are applicable not only to the Only-begotten, but to everyone who in and like Jesus is called a son of God.

The simple truth and force of the illustration is seen in Jesus with His earthly father in the carpenter's shop learning his trade. The first thing you notice is the entire *dependence*: "The Son can do nothing of himself, but what he seeth the Father do." Then you are struck by the implicit *obedience* that seeks to imitate the Father: "For what things soever he doeth, these also doeth the Son likewise." You then notice the loving *intimacy* to which the Father admits Him, keeping back none of His secrets: "For the Father loveth the Son, and showeth him

83

all things that himself doeth." And in this dependent obedience on His Son's part, and the loving teaching on the Father's part, you have the pledge of an ever-growing *advance* to greater works: step by step the Son will be led up to all that the Father himself can do: "He will show him greater works than these, that ye may marvel."

In this picture we have the reflection of the relationship between God the Father and the Son in His blessed humanity. If His humanity is to be something real and true, and if we are to understand how Christ is to be our example, we must believe fully in what our Lord here reveals to us of the secrets of His inner life. The words He speaks are literal truth. His dependence on the Father for each moment of His life was absolutely and intensely real: "The Son can do nothing of himself, but what he seeth the Father do." He counted it no humiliation to wait on Him for His commands: He rather considered it His highest blessedness to be led and guided of the Father as a child. And accordingly He held himself bound in strictest obedience to say and do only what the Father showed Him: "What things soever he doeth, these also doeth the Son likewise."

The proof of this is the exceeding carefulness with which He sought to live according to Holy Scripture. In His sufferings He will endure all in order that the Scriptures may be fulfilled. For this He remained the whole night in prayer. In such continued prayer He presents His thought to the Father, and waits for the answer, that He may know the Father's will. No child nor slave was ever so anxious to keep to what the father or master had said as Jesus was to follow the teaching and guidance of His heavenly Father. On this account the Father kept nothing hid from Him: the entire dependence and willingness to always learn were rewarded with the most perfect communication of all the Father's secrets. "For the Father loveth the Son, and showeth him all things . . . and will show him greater works than these, that ye may marvel." The Father had formed a glorious life plan for the Son, that in Him the divine life might be manifested in the conditions of human existence: this plan was shown to the Son step by step until at last all was gloriously accomplished.

Child of God, it was not only for the only-begotten Son that a life plan was arranged, but for each of His children. In proportion to our dependence on the Father will this life plan be more or less perfectly worked out in our lives. The nearer the believer comes to this entire dependence of the Son, "doing nothing but what he sees the Father do," and then to His implicit obedience, "whatsoever he doeth, doing these in like manner," so much more will the promise be fulfilled to us: "The Father showeth him all things that he himself doeth, and will show him greater works than these." *Like Christ!* That word calls us to a life of conformity to the Son in His blessed dependence on the Father. Each of us is invited to live like Him.

This dependence on the Father is first of all founded upon the faith that He will make His will known to us. Many do not believe that the Lord cares for them enough to daily teach them and to make known His will just as He did to Jesus. Believer, you are of more value to the Father than you realize. You are worth as much as the price He paid—that is, the blood of His Son. He therefore attaches the highest value to your smallest concerns and will guide even in what seems insignificant. He longs more for a close relationship with you than you can conceive. He can use you for His glory, and make of you something higher than you can understand. The Father loves His child, and shows him what He does. That He proved in Jesus; and He will prove it in us too. There must only be the surrender to expect His teaching. Through His Holy Spirit He gives this most tenderly. Without removing us from others, the Father can so conform us to Christ's image that we will be a blessing and joy to all. Do not allow unbelief of God's compassionate love to prevent you from expecting the Father's guidance in all things.

The second great hindrance is an unwillingness to submit yourself to Him. The desire for independence was the temptation in paradise and is the temptation in each human heart. Yet, it is this dependence which brings us into most blessed communion with God: it becomes true of us as of Jesus, "The Father loveth the Son, and showeth him all things that himself doeth." This dependence takes from us all care and responsibility: we have only to obey orders. It gives real power and strength of will, because we know that He works in us to will and to do. It gives us the blessed assurance that our work will succeed, because we have allowed God alone to take charge of it.

If you have not known this life of conscious dependence and simple obedience, begin today. Let your Savior be your example in this. It is His will to live in you, and in you to be again what He was here on earth. He longs for your consent: He will work it in you. Offer yourself to the Father, to do nothing of yourself but only what the Father shows you. Fix your gaze on Jesus as the example and promise of what you shall be. Adore Him who, for your sake, humbled himself and showed how blessed the dependent life can be.

Blessed dependence! It is our only proper attitude toward such a God. It gives Him the glory which belongs to Him as God. It keeps the soul in peace and rest, for it allows God to care for all. It keeps the mind quiet and prepared to receive and use the Father's teaching. And it is gloriously rewarded in deeper experiences with himself and ever-advancing discoveries of His will and work.

Blessed dependence! It was because Jesus knew that He was *a Son* that He thus loved to be dependent on *the Father*. Of all the teaching in regard to the likeness of Christ, this is central: I must live as a Son with my Father. If I stand clear in this relationship, *as a son, realizing that the Father is everything to me*, a sonlike life, living through the Father and for the Father, will be its natural and spontaneous outcome.

O my Father, the longer I fix my gaze upon the image of the Son, the more I discover how far sin has separated me from you. To be dependent upon you: there can be no higher blessing than this: to trust in all things in a God such as you are, so wise and good, so rich and powerful. Yet, it seems so difficult; we would rather be dependent on our own folly than the God of all glory. Even your own children, O most blessed Father, often think it so hard to give up their own thoughts and will, and to believe that absolute dependence on God, even to the most insignificant things, is alone true blessedness.

Lord, I humbly come to you: teach me this. He who purchased with His own blood for me the everlasting blessedness has shown me in His own life wherein that blessedness consists. And I know He will now lead and keep me in it. O my Father! I yield myself to you, to be made like Him—like Him to do nothing of myself, but what I see you doing. Father, take me too, like the First-born, into your training and show me what you are doing. O my God, be a Father to me as you were to Christ and let me be your son as He was! Amen.

16

In His Love

"A new commandment I give unto you, That ye love one another; as I have loved you, that ye also love one another" (John 13:34).

"This is my commandment, That ye love one another, as I have loved you" (John 15:12).

Even as: Have we begun to understand some of the blessedness of that little word? This is not the command of a law which only convinces of sin and impotence; it is a new command under a new covenant and is established upon better promises. It is the command of Him who asks nothing that He has not provided. It is the assurance that He expects nothing from us that He does not work in us: *even as* I have loved you, and every moment am pouring out that love upon you through the Holy Spirit, *even so* do you love one another. The measure, the strength, and the work of your love you will find only in Christ's love to you.

Even as I have loved you: that word gives us the *measure* of the love with which we must love each other. True love knows no measure: it gives itself entirely. It may take into consideration the time and measure of showing it; but love itself is ever whole and undivided. This is the greatest glory of divine love that we have. This is the glory of the love of Jesus, who is the image of God, that He loves us even as the Father loves Him.

And this is the glory of brotherly love, that it will know of no other law than to love even as God and Christ.

He who would be like Christ must unhesitatingly accept this as his rule of life. He knows how difficult, how impossible it often is to love the brethren, in whom there seems so much that is offensive or unamiable. Before meeting them in the strength of his own love, he goes in secret to the Lord and with his eye fixed on his own sin and unworthiness asks: How much do I owe you? He goes to the cross and seeks there to fathom the love wherewith the Lord has loved him. He lets the light of the immeasurable love of Christ to shine in upon his soul until he learns to feel that divine love has but one law: love seeks not its own; love gives itself wholly. And he lays himself on the altar before his Lord: even as you loved me, so will I love the brethren. In virtue of my union with Jesus, there can be no question of anything less: I love them as Christ did. Oh, that believers would close their ears to all the reasonings of their own hearts and fix their eyes on the law which He who loves them has promulgated in His own example. They would soon realize that there is nothing for them to do but this—to accept His commands and to obey them.

Our love must be measured only by His, because His love is *the strength* of ours. The love of Christ is no mere idea or sentiment; it is a real divine life power. As long as the Christian does not understand this, it cannot exert its full power in him. But when his faith rises to realize that Christ's love is nothing less than the imparting of himself and His love to the beloved, then he sees that his Lord simply asks that he should allow His love to flow through him. He must live in a Christ-given strength: the love of Christ constrains him and enables him to love as He did.

From this love of Christ the believer also learns what *the work* of his love to the brethren must be. We have already spoken of many manifestations of love: its loving service, its self-denial, its meekness. Love is the root of all these. It teaches the disciple to look upon himself as really called upon to be, in his little circle, just like Jesus, the one who lives solely to love and help others. Paul prays for the Philippians: "That your love may abound yet more and more in knowledge and in all judgment" (Phil. 1:9). Love does not immediately comprehend what the work is that it can do. The believer who prays that his love may abound in knowledge, and takes Christ's example as his rule of life, will be taught what a great and glorious work there is for him to do. The Church of God, and every child of God, as well as the world, has an unspeakable need of love, of the manifestation of Christ's love. The believer who takes the Lord's word, "Love one another, as I have loved you," as a command that must be obeyed carries about a power for blessing and life for all with whom he comes in contact. Love is the only explanation of the life of Christ, and of the wonder of His death: divine love in God's children will still work its mighty wonders.

"Behold what manner of love!" "Behold how he loved!" These words are the superscription over the love of the Father and of the Son. They must yet become the keywords to the life of every believer. They will be so where in living faith and true consecration the command of Christ to love is accepted as the law of life. As early as the call of Abraham this principle was deposited as a living seed in God's kingdom, that what God is for us, we must be for others. "I will bless thee . . . and thou shalt be a blessing" (Gen. 12:2). If "I have loved you" is the highest manifestation of what God is for us, then "even so love ye" must be the highest expression of what the child of God must be. In preaching, as in the life of the Church, it must be understood: *The love which loves like Christ is the sign of true discipleship.*

Beloved! Christ Jesus longs to make you a very fountain of love. The love of heaven desires possession of you in order that in and through you it may work its blessed work on earth. Yield to its rule. Offer yourself unreservedly to its indwelling. Honor it by the confident assurance that it can teach you to love as Jesus loved. As conformity to the Lord Jesus must be the chief mark of your life, so love must be the chief mark of that conformity. Be not disheartened if you do not attain it at once. Only hold fast the command, "Love, even as I have loved you." It takes time to grow into it. Take time in secret to gaze on that image of love. Take time in prayer and meditation to fan the desire into a burning flame. Take time to survey all around you, whoever they may be and whatever may happen, with this one thought: "I must love them." Take time to become conscious of your union with Christ, that every fear as to the possibility of thus loving may be met with the word: "Have not I commanded you: Love as I have loved"? Take time in loving communion with Jesus and you will joyfully fulfill this command, too, to love even as He did.

Lord Jesus, you have loved me so wonderfully, and now you command me to love like you. Behold me at your feet. Joyfully I accept your command, and go out in your strength to manifest your love to all.

In your strength, O my Lord, be therefore pleased to reveal your love to me. Shed abroad your love in my heart through the Holy Spirit. Let me live each moment in the experience that I am the beloved of God.

Lord, let me understand that I can love, not with my own, but with your love. You live in me, your Spirit dwells and works in me; from you there streams into me the love with which I can love others. I surrender myself to live as you lived. I look upon my old self with its selfishness and unlovingness as crucified, and in faith prepare to do as you say.

Lord, I do it. In the strength of my Lord, I live *to love even as you have loved me*. Amen.

17

In His Praying

"And in the morning, rising up a great while before day, he went out, and departed into a solitary place, and there prayed" (Mark 1:35).

"And he said unto them, Come ye yourselves apart into a desert place, and rest a while" (Mark 6:31).

In His life of prayer, my Savior is also my example. He could not maintain the heavenly life in His soul without continually separating himself from man and communing with His Father. With the heavenly life in me, it is the same: it has the same need for being separate from man long enough to have true communion with the Father in heaven.

Mark records in his gospel the commencement of Jesus' public ministry that so stirred the area of Capernaum (Mark 1). After a day full of wonders and work (vv. 21–32), the demands in the evening became still greater. The whole town is before the door; the sick are healed and demons are cast out. It is late before they get to sleep; in the throng there is little time for quiet or for private prayer. As the disciples rise in the morning, they find Jesus gone. In the silence of the very early morning, He has gone out to seek a place of quietness in the wilderness; when they find Him, He is still praying.

And why did He need these hours of prayer? Did He not know the blessedness of silently lifting up His soul to God in the midst of the most pressing business? Did not the Father dwell in Him? and did He not in the depth of His heart enjoy unbroken communion with Him? Yes. But that life, as subject to the law of humanity, had need of continual refreshing and renewing from the fountain. It was a life of dependence; just because it was strong and true, it could not bear the loss of direct and constant communion with the Father, with whom and in whom it had its being and its blessedness.

What a lesson for every believer! Prolonged relationships with others is dissipating and dangerous to our spiritual life: it brings us under the influence of the visible and temporal. Nothing can atone for the loss of private and direct communion with God. Even work in the service of God and of love is exhausting: we cannot bless others without power going out from us; this must be renewed from above. The law of the necessity of the manna from heaven still holds true. Jesus Christ taught us by His example. My life is like His, a life hid in heaven, in God; it needs time daily to be fed from heaven. It is *from heaven* alone that the power to lead *a heavenly life* on earth can come.

And what may have occupied our Lord so long in prayer? If I could hear Him pray, I would know how I too must pray! God be praised! of His prayers more than one is recorded, that in them too we might learn to follow His example. In the high-priestly prayer (John 17), we hear Him speak, as in the deep calm of heaven, to His Father; in His Gethsemane prayer, a few hours later, we see Him call out of the depths of trouble and darkness unto God. In these two prayers we have the highest and the deepest there is to be found in the communion of prayer between Father and Son.

In both prayers we see how He addresses God. Each time it is *Father! O my Father!* That word holds the secret of all prayer. The Lord knew that He was a Son and that the Father loved Him: with that word He placed himself in the full light of the Father's countenance. This was to Him the greatest need and greatest blessing of prayer, to enter into the full enjoyment of the Father's love. It must be the same with us. Prayer should principally be the holy silence and adoration of faith in which I wait upon God until He reveals himself to me, until He gives me through His Spirit the loving assurance that He looks upon me as a Father, that I am well pleasing to Him. He who has not time in quietness of soul, and in full consciousness of its meaning, to say *Abba Father* has missed the best part of prayer. It is in prayer that the witness of the Spirit that we are children of God, and that the Father draws nigh and delights in us, must be exercised and strengthened. "If our heart condemn us not, we have confidence toward God; and whatsoever we ask, we receive of him, because we obey his commandments, and do the things that are pleasing in his sight."

In both prayers I also see what He desired: *that the Father may be glorified*. He speaks: "I have glorified thee; glorify thy Son, that thy Son *also may glorify thee*." That reflects the spirit of every prayer of Jesus; the entire surrender of himself to live only for the Father's will and glory. All that He asked had but one object, "that God might be glorified." In this too He is my example. I must seek this same spirit in every prayer: Father, bless your child and glorify your grace in me that your child may glorify you. Everything in the universe was designed to manifest God's glory. The believer who is inspired with this thought, and avails himself in prayer to receive and express it, will have power in prayer. Even of His work in heaven our Lord says: "Whatsoever ye shall ask in my name, that will I do, *that the Father may be glorified in the Son*." O my soul, learn from the Savior to first yield yourself as a whole burnt offering, with the one object that God may be glorified in you.

This is the only sure ground on which to pray. You will feel the strong desire and the full liberty to ask the Father that in each part of Christ's example you may be made like Him, so God may be glorified. You will understand how the soul must wait upon God to work in it what will be to His glory. Because Jesus surrendered himself so entirely to the glory of His Father, He was worthy to be our Mediator and could in His high-priestly prayer ask such great blessings for His people. Learn like Jesus only to seek God's glory in prayer, and you will become an intercessor who not only approaches the throne of grace with his own needs, but can also pray for others the effectual fervent prayer of a righteous man that avails much. The words which the Savior put into our mouth in the Lord's Prayer, "Thy will be done," become ours in the power of His atonement and intercession. We too become Christlike in that priestly intercession on which the unity and prosperity of the Church and the salvation of sinners so much depend.

And he, whose every prayer is for God's glory, will also have strength for the prayer of Gethsemane, if God calls him to it. Every prayer of Christ was intercession, because He had given himself for us; all He asked and received was in our interest; every prayer He prayed was in the spirit of self-sacrifice. Give yourself wholly to God for others. This is the only preparation for those single hours of soul struggle in which we may be called to some special act of the surrender of the will that costs us tears and anguish. But he who has learned the former will surely receive strength for the latter.

O my brother, if you and I would be like Jesus, we must especially consider Jesus praying alone in the wilderness. *There is the secret of His wonderful life.* What He did and spoke to man *was first spoken and lived through with the Father.* In communion with Him, the anointing with the Holy Spirit was daily renewed. He who would be like Jesus must simply begin here—follow Jesus into solitude. Though it cost the sacrifice of sleep, of business, of relationships with friends, *the time must be found to be alone with the Father.* Besides the ordinary time of prayer, he will feel at times irresistibly drawn to enter into the holy place and to remain there until he is completely renewed in spirit. In his private place, or in the solitude of the wilderness, God must be found every day and our fellowship with Him renewed. If Christ needed it, how much more we! What it was to Him it will be much more for us.

What it was to Him is apparent from what is written of His baptism: "It came to pass, that Jesus also being baptized *and praying,* the heaven was opened, and the Holy Ghost descended in a bodily shape like a dove upon him, and a voice came from heaven, which said, Thou art my beloved Son, in thee I am well pleased" (Luke 3:21, 22). Yes, this will be to us the blessing of prayer: the opened heaven, the baptism of the Spirit, the Father's voice, the blessed assurance of His love and good pleasure. *As with Jesus, so with us; from above it must come in answer to prayer.*

Christlike praying in private will be the secret of Christlike living in public. Oh, let us rise and avail ourselves of our wonderful privilege—the Christlike boldness of access into the Father's presence, the Christlike liberty with God in prayer.

O my blessed Lord, you called me and I have followed you that I may bear your image in all things. Daily I seek your footsteps that I may follow wherever you go. This day your footsteps, wet with the dew of night, led to the wilderness. There I have seen you kneeling for hours before the Father. There I have heard you yield yourself to the Father's glory and from the Father you asked and received all that was needed in your life. Impress this wonderful vision deep in my soul: my Savior rising a great while before day to seek communion with the Father, asking and obtaining all that He needed for His life and work.

O my Lord! who am I that I may listen to you? Who am I that you call me to pray, even as you have done? Precious Savior, from the depths of my heart I beseech you, awaken in me the same strong need of private prayer. Deeply convince me that the divine life cannot attain its full growth without this private communion with my heavenly Father, so that my soul may indeed dwell in the light of His countenance. Let this conviction awaken in me such burning desire that I may not rest until my soul has been daily baptized in the streams of heavenly love. Jesus, teach me to pray like you. Amen.

18

In His Use of Scripture

"That all things must be fulfilled, which were written in the law of Moses, and in the prophets, and in the psalms, concerning me" (Luke 24:44).

What the Lord Jesus accomplished here on earth as a man He owed greatly to His use of the Scriptures. He found in them the way marked in which He was to walk, the food and the strength by which He could work, the weapon by which He overcame every enemy. The Scriptures were indeed indispensable to Him throughout His life and passion: from beginning to end His life was the fulfillment of what had been written of Him in the volume of the Book.

It is hardly necessary to attempt proving this. In the temptation in the wilderness it was by His *"It is written"* that He conquered Satan. In His conflicts with the Pharisees He continually appealed to the Word: *"What saith the Scripture?" "Have ye not read?" "Is it not written?"* With His disciples it was always from the Scriptures that He proved the certainty and necessity of His sufferings and resurrection: *"How otherwise can the Scriptures be fulfilled?"* And, with His Father in His last sufferings, it is in the words of Scripture that He pours out the complaint of being forsaken, and then again commends His spirit into the Father's hands. All this has a very deep meaning. He himself was the living Word. He had the Spirit without measure. If anyone could ever have done without the written Word, it was Jesus. And yet we see that it was everything to Him. He demonstrated that *the life of God in human flesh and the word of God in human speech* are inseparably connected. Jesus would not have been what He was, could not have done what He did, had He not yielded himself step by step to be led and sustained by the Word of God.

The Word of God is called seed; it is the seed of the divine life. We know what seed is. It is that wonderful organism in which the life, the invisible essence of a plant or tree, is so concentrated and embodied that it can be taken away and made available to impart the life of the tree elsewhere. This use may be twofold. As fruit we eat it, for instance, in the corn that gives us bread; and the life of the plant becomes our nourishment and our life. Or we plant it, and the life of the plant reproduces and multiplies itself. In both aspects the Word of God is seed.

True life is found only in God. But that life must have a means to be imparted to us. It is in the Word of God that the divine life takes shape, and brings itself within our reach, and becomes communicable. The life, the thoughts, the feelings, the power of God are embodied in His words. And it is only through His Word that the life of God can really enter into us. His Word is the seed of the heavenly life.

As the bread of life we eat it, we feed upon it. In eating our daily bread, the body takes in the nourishment which nature prepared for us in the seed corn. We assimilate it, and it becomes our very own, part of ourselves; it is our life. In feeding upon the Word of God, the powers of the heavenly life enter into us and become our very own—the life of our life.

Or we use the seed to plant. The words of God are sown in our heart. They have a divine power of reproduction and multiplication. The very life that is in them, the divine thought, or disposition, or powers that each of them contains, takes root in the believing heart and grows up; and the very thing of which the word was the expression is produced within us. The words of God are the seeds of the fullness of the divine life.

The Lord Jesus was entirely dependent upon the Word of God and submitted himself wholly to it. His mother taught

Him. The teachers of Nazareth instructed Him in it. In meditation and prayer, in the exercise of obedience and faith, He was led, during His years of preparation, to understand and appropriate it. The Word of the Father was to the Son the life of His soul. What He said in the wilderness was spoken from His inmost personal experience: "Man shall not live by bread alone, but by every word that proceedeth out of the mouth of God" (Matt. 4:4). He felt He could not live unless the Word brought Him the life of the Father. The Word was to Him not instead of the Father, but the vehicle for the living fellowship with the living God. And He had His whole mind and heart so filled with it that the Holy Spirit could at each moment find within Him the right word to suggest just as He needed it.

If you would become a man of God, strong in faith, full of blessing, rich in fruit to the glory of God, be full of the Word of God. Like Christ, make the Word your bread. Let it dwell richly in you. Have your heart full of it. Feed on it. Believe it. Obey it. It is only by believing and obeying that the Word can enter into our inward parts, into our very being. Take it daily as the Word that is proceeding out of the mouth of God, as the Word of the living God, who in it holds living fellowship with His children and speaks to them in living power. Take your thoughts of God's will, and God's work, and God's purpose with you. The Word taught you by the Father will enable you to fulfill all that is written in the Scripture concerning you.

In Christ's use of Scripture the most remarkable thing is this: *He found himself there; He saw there His own image and likeness.* And He gave himself to the fulfillment of what He found written there. It was this that encouraged Him under the bitterest sufferings, and strengthened Him for the most difficult work. Everywhere He saw traced by God's own hand the divine way: *through suffering to glory.* He had but one thought: to be what the Father had said He should be, to have His life correspond exactly to the image of what He should be as He found it in the Word of God.

In the Scriptures *our likeness too is to be found,* a picture of what the Father means us to be. Seek to have a deep and clear impression of what the Father says in His Word that you should be. If this is fully understood, it is inconceivable what courage it will give to conquer every difficulty. To know: it is ordained of God; I have seen what has been written concerning me in God's book; I have seen the image of what I am called in God's counsel to be. This thought inspires the soul with a faith that conquers the world.

The Lord Jesus found His own image not only in the institutions, but especially in the believers of the Old Testament. Moses, Aaron, Joshua, David and the prophets were types. And so He himself is the image of believers in the New Testament. It is in *Him and His example* that we find our own image in the Scriptures. "To be changed into the same image, from glory to glory, by the Spirit of the Lord," we must in the Scripture-glass gaze on that image as our own. The Spirit teaches us to take Christ as our example and to gaze on every feature as the promise of what can be.

Blessed is the believer who has not only found Jesus in the Scriptures but also in His image the promise and example of what he is to become. Blessed is the believer who yields himself to be taught by the Holy Spirit to not dilute the Scriptures but in simplicity to accept what it reveals of God's thoughts about His children.

It was "according to the Scriptures" that Jesus Christ lived and died; it was "according to the Scriptures" that He was raised again: all that the Scriptures said He must do or suffer He was able to accomplish because He knew and obeyed them. All that the Scriptures had promised that the Father should do for Him, the Father did. Give yourself with an undivided heart to learn in the Scriptures what God says concerning you. Let the Scriptures in which Jesus found the food for His daily life be your daily food and meditation. Go to God's Word with the joyful and confident expectation that through the blessed Spirit, the Word will indeed accomplish its divine purpose in you. Every word of God is full of a divine life and power. Be assured that when you use the Scriptures as Christ used them, they will do for you what they did for Him. God has marked out the plan for your life in His Word; each day you will find some portion of it there. Nothing makes a man more strong and courageous than the

---

assurance that he is obeying the will of God.

O Lord, my God! Thank you for your precious Word, the divine glass of all unseen and eternal realities. I thank you that I have in it the image of your Son, who is your image, and also my image. I thank you that as I gaze on Him I may also see what I can be.

O my Father, teach me to understand what a blessing your Word can bring me. To your Son it was the manifestation of your will, the communication of your life and strength, the fellowship with yourself. In the acceptance and the surrender to your Word, He was able to fulfill all your counsel. May your Word be all this to me too. Make it to me, daily through the power of the Holy Spirit, the Word proceeding from your mouth, the voice of your living presence speaking to me. May I feel with each word that it is God coming to impart to me something of His own life. Teach me to keep it hidden in my heart as a divine seed, which in its own time will spring up and produce in me in divine reality the very life that was hid in it, the very thing which I at first saw only as a thought. Teach me above all to find in it Him who is its center and substance the eternal Word. Finding Him, and myself in Him, I shall learn like Him to count your Word my food and my life.

I ask this, O my God, in the name of our blessed Christ Jesus. Amen.

19

In Forgiving

"Forbearing one another, and forgiving one another, if any man have a quarrel against any: even as Christ forgave you, so also do ye" (Col. 3:13).

Forgiveness is one of the first and most glorious blessings we receive from God. It is the transition from the old to the new life; the sign and pledge of God's love: with it we receive the right to all the spiritual gifts which are prepared for us in Christ. The believer can never forget, either here or in eternity, that he is a forgiven sinner. Nothing more inflames his love, awakens his joy, or strengthens his courage than the continually renewed experience of God's forgiving love. Every day, yes, every thought of God reminds him: I owe all to pardoning grace.

This forgiving love is one of the greatest manifestations of the divine nature. In it God finds His glory and blessedness and wants to share this with His redeemed people. He calls upon them also to bestow forgiveness upon others.

Have you ever noticed how often and how expressly the Lord Jesus spoke of it? If we read Matt. 6:12, 15; 18:2–25; Mark 11:25, we shall understand how inseparably the two are united: God's forgiveness of us and our forgiveness of others. After the Lord ascended to grant repentance and forgiveness of sins, the Scriptures say, *"Even as Christ* has forgiven you, *so also do ye."* We must be like God, like Christ, in forgiving.

It is not difficult to find the reason for this. When forgiving love comes to us, it is not only to deliver us from punishment. No, much more; it seeks to win us for its own, to take possession of us and to dwell in us. And when it has come to dwell in us, it does not lose its own heavenly character and beauty: it still is forgiving love seeking to do its work in us and through us, leading and enabling us to forgive those who sin against us. This is so much the case that we are told that not to forgive is a sure sign one has himself not been forgiven. To seek only forgiveness as freedom from punishment and to not truly receive forgiving love to rule his heart and life proves that God's forgiveness has never really reached him. He who has truly received forgiveness will have in the joy with which he forgives others, a continual confirmation that his faith in God's forgiveness of himself is a reality. *From Christ* to receive forgiveness, and *like Christ* to bestow it on others: these two are one.

This is clearly the teaching of Scripture. But what do the lives and experiences of believers say? Alas! many hardly know that it is so written; others know it, but think it is more than can be expected from them; others agree in general to what has been said, but always find a reason, in their own particular case, why it should not be so. The excuses are unending. And yet the command is so very simple and its sanction so very solemn: "Even as Christ has forgiven you, so also do ye"; "If ye forgive not, neither will your Father forgive you." With such human reasonings, the Word of God is nullified. As though it were not just through forgiving love that God seeks to conquer evil, and therefore forgives even unto seventy times seven. It is clearly not what the offender would do to me *but what Christ has done* that must be the rule of my conduct. As though conformity to the example not of Christ himself, but of other believers, were the sign that I have truly received the forgiveness of sins.

Where is the church or Christian circle in which the law of forgiving love is not grievously transgressed? How often in our church assemblies, in ordinary social relationships, and even in domestic life, proof is given that to many the call to forgive has not become a ruling principle in their conduct. On account of a difference of opinion, or opposition to a course of action that appeared to us right, on the ground of a real or an imagined humiliation or the report of some unkind or thoughtless word, feelings of resentment, or contempt, or separation, have been harbored, instead of loving, and forgiving, and forgetting like Christ. The thought has never yet taken possession of mind and heart, that the law of compassion and love and forgiveness, in which the relation of the head to the members is rooted, must rule all relationships of the members to each other.

We must learn that as forgiveness of our sins was one of the first things Jesus did for us, forgiveness of others is one of the first that we can do for Him. To the new heart there is a joy even sweeter than that of being forgiven—the forgiving of others. The joy of being forgiven is only that of a sinner and of earth: the joy of forgiving is Christ's own joy, the joy of heaven. Oh, come and see that it is nothing less than the work that Christ himself does, and the joy with which He himself is satisfied that you are called to participate in.

Here you can bless the world. It is as the forgiving One that Jesus conquers His enemies and binds His friends to himself. It is as the forgiving One that Jesus has set up His kingdom and continually extends it. It is through the same forgiving love, not only preached but *shown in the life of His disciples*, that the Church will convince the world of God's love. If the world sees men and women loving and forgiving as Jesus did, it will be compelled to confess that God is truly with them.

And if it still seems too hard and too high, remember that this is only a reflection from the natural heart. It has no taste for this joy and can never attain it. But in union with Christ we can do it: He who abides in Him walks even as He walked. If you have surrendered yourself to follow Christ in everything, then He will by His Spirit enable you to do this too. Fix your gaze on Jesus, in the heavenly beauty of His forgiving love as your example: "Beholding the glory of the Lord, we are changed into the same image, from glory to glory." Every time you pray or thank God for forgiveness, declare that to the glory of His name you will manifest the same forgiving love to all around you. Before there is a question of forgiveness of others, let your heart be filled with love to Christ, love to the brethren, and love to enemies: a heart full of love finds it blessed to forgive. In each circumstance where the temptation to not forgive arises, allow it to be the opportunity to show how truly you live in God's forgiving love, how glad you are to let its beautiful light shine through you on others, and how blessed a privilege you feel it to be to bear the image of your beloved Lord.

To forgive like you, blessed Son of God! I take this as the law of my life. You who have given the command will also give the power. You who loved enough to forgive me will also fill me with love and teach me to forgive others. You who gave me the first blessing, in the joy of having my sins forgiven, will surely give me the second blessing, the deeper joy of forgiving others as you have forgiven me. Oh, fill me with faith in the power of your love in me to make me like yourself, to enable me to forgive the seventy times seven, and so to love and bless all around me.

O my Jesus! your example is my law: I must be like you. And your example is my gospel too: I can be as you are. What you demand of me by your example, you work in me by your life. I shall forgive like you.

Lord, lead me deeper into my dependence on you, into the all sufficiency of your grace and the blessed keeping which comes from your indwelling. Then shall I believe and prove the all-prevailing power of love. I shall forgive even as Christ has forgiven me. Amen.

20

In Beholding Him

"But we all, with open face beholding as in a glass the glory of the Lord, are changed into the same image, from glory to glory, even as by the Spirit of the Lord" (2 Cor. 3:18).

Moses had been forty days on the mount in communion with God. When he came down, his face shone with divine glory. He did not know it himself, but Aaron and the people saw it (Ex. 34:30). It was so evidently God's glory that Aaron and the people feared to approach him.

In this we have an image of what takes place in the New Testament. The privilege that Moses alone enjoyed is now the portion of every believer. When we behold the glory of God in Christ, in the glass of the Holy Scriptures, His glory shines upon us and into us and fills us until it shines out from us. By gazing on His glory, the believer is changed through the Spirit into the same image. *Beholding Jesus makes us like Him.*

It is a law of nature that the eye exercises a profound influence on mind and character. The education of a child is carried on greatly through the eye; he is molded very much by the manners and habits of those he sees. To form and mold our character the heavenly Father shows us His divine glory in the face of Jesus. He does it in the expectation that it will give us great joy to gaze upon it, and because He knows that, gazing on it we shall be conformed to the same image. Let everyone who desires to be like Jesus note how he can attain it.

Look continually to the divine glory as seen in Christ. What is the special characteristic of the glory? *It is the manifestation of divine perfection in human form.* The chief marks of the image of the divine glory in Christ are these two: His humiliation and His love.

There is the glory of His humiliation. When you see how the eternal Son emptied himself and became man, and how as man He humbled himself as a servant and was obedient even unto the death of the cross, you have seen the highest glory of God. The glory of God's omnipotence as Creator and the glory of God's holiness as King is not so amazing as this: the glory of grace which humbled itself as a servant to serve God and man. We must learn to look upon this humiliation as real glory. *To be humbled like Christ must be to us the only thing worthy of the name of glory on earth.* It must become in our eyes the most beautiful, the most wonderful, the most desirable thing that can be imagined—a very joy to look upon or think of. The effect of gazing upon it and admiring it will be that you will not be able to conceive of any glory greater than to be and act like Jesus, and will long to humble yourself even as He did. Gazing on Jesus, admiring and adoring Him, will work in us the same mind that there was in Him, and so we shall be changed into His image.

Inseparable from this is the glory of His love. The humiliation leads you back to the love as its origin and power. It is from love that the humiliation has its beauty. Love is the highest glory of God. But this love was a hidden mystery until it was manifest in Christ Jesus. It is only in His humanity, in His gentle, compassionate, and loving relationships with foolish, sinful, hostile men that the glory of divine love was fully seen. The soul that gets a glimpse of this glory, that understands that *to love like Christ is alone worthy of the name of glory,* will long to become like Christ in this. Beholding this glory of the love of God in Christ, he is changed into the same image.

Would you be like Christ? Here is the path. Gaze on the glory of God in Him. *In Him,* that is to say; do not look only to the words and the thoughts and the graces in which His glory is seen, but look to *Him*, the living, loving Christ. Behold Him, look into His eyes, look into His face, as a loving friend, as the living God.

Look to Him in adoration. Bow before Him as God. His glory has an almighty living power to impart itself to us, to pass over into us and to fill us.

Look to Him in faith. Exercise the blessed trust that He is yours, that He has given himself to you, and that you have a claim to all that is in Him. It is His purpose to work His image in you. Behold Him with the joyful and certain expectation: the glory that I behold in Him is destined for me. He will give it to me; as I gaze and trust, I become like Christ.

Look to Him with strong desire. Do not yield to the sloth-fulness of the flesh that is satisfied without the full blessing of conformity to the Lord. Pray the Lord will free you from all carnal contentment with present attainments, and to fill you with the unquenchable longing for His glory. Pray most fervently the prayer of Moses, "Show me thy glory." Let nothing discourage you, not even the apparently slow progress you make, but press on with an ever-growing desire for the blessed prospect that God's Word holds out to you: "We are changed into the same image, from glory to glory."

And as you behold Him, above all, let the look of love not be lacking. Tell Him continually how He has won your heart, how you do love Him, how entirely you belong to Him. Tell Him that to please Him, the beloved One, is your highest, your only joy. Let the bond of love between you and Him be drawn continually closer. Love unites.

Like Christ! We can be it, we shall be it, each in our measure. The Holy Spirit is the pledge that it shall be. God's Word has said, "We are changed into the same image, from glory to glory, even as by *the Spirit of the Lord*." This is the Spirit that was in Jesus, and through whom the divine glory lived and shone. This Spirit is called "The Spirit of glory." This Spirit is in us as in the Lord Jesus, and it is His work to bring into us and work within us what we see in our Lord Jesus. Through this Spirit we have already Christ's life in us, with all the gifts of His grace. But that life must be stirred up and developed: it must grow, penetrate into our whole being, take possession of our entire personality. We can count on the Spirit to work this in us if we but yield ourselves to Him and obey Him. As we gaze on Jesus in the Word, He opens our eyes to see the glory of all that Jesus does and is. He makes us willing to be like Him. He strengthens our faith. He works in us unceasingly the life of abiding in Christ, a wholehearted union and communion with Him. He does according to the promise: "The Spirit shall glorify me: for he shall take of mine and shall show it unto you." We are changed into the image on which we gaze from glory to glory, *as by the Spirit of the Lord.* Let us only understand that the fullness of the Spirit is freely given to us. He who surrenders himself to be filled with the Spirit will experience how gloriously He accomplishes His work of stamping on our souls and lives the image and likeness of Christ.

Beholding Jesus and His glory, you can confidently expect to become like Him: only trust yourself in quietness and rest of soul to the leading of the Spirit. *"The Spirit of glory rests upon you."* Gaze on and adore the glory of God in Christ; you will be changed with divine power from glory to glory; in the power of the Holy Spirit the mighty transformation will be accomplished, and *like Christ* will be the God-given experience of your life.

My Lord, I do thank you for the glorious assurance that while I behold your glory, the Holy Spirit is changing me into that image of your glory.

Lord, grant me to truly behold your glory. Moses had been forty days with you when your glory shone upon him. I acknowledge that my communion with you has been too short and passing, that I have taken too little time to come under the full impression of what your image is. Lord, teach me this. Draw me in my meditations to surrender myself to contemplate and adore until my soul at every line of that image may exclaim: This is glorious! this is the glory of God! O my God, show me your glory!

And strengthen my faith, blessed Lord, that, even when I am not conscious of any special experience, the Holy Spirit will do His work. Moses knew not that his face shone. Lord, keep me from looking at self. May I be so taken up with you as to forget and lose myself in you. Lord, it is he who is dead to self who lives in you.

O my Lord, as often as I gaze upon your image and your example, I would do it in the faith that the Holy Spirit will fill me, will take entire possession of me, and so work your likeness in me that the world may see in me something of your glory. In this faith I will venture to take your precious word, *"from glory to glory,"* as my watchword, to be to me the promise of a grace that grows richer every day. Your blessing is ever ready to surpass itself and to make what has been given only the pledge of the better that is to come. Precious Savior! gazing on you it shall indeed be so, "from glory to glory." Amen.

21

In His Humility

"In lowliness of mind let each esteem other better than themselves. . . . Let this mind be in you, which was also in Christ Jesus, who being in the form of God . . . made himself of no reputation, and took upon him the form of a servant, and was made in the likeness of men: and being found in fashion as a man, he humbled himself, and became obedient unto death, even the death of the cross" (Phil. 2:3–8).

This wonderful passage includes a summary of the most precious truths that surround the person of Christ. There is first, His adorable divinity: *"in the form of God," "equal with God."* Then comes the mystery of His incarnation, in that word of deep and inexhaustible meaning: *"He emptied himself—made himself of no reputation."* The atonement follows, with the humiliation, and obedience, and suffering, and death, from which it derives its worth: *"He humbled himself, and became obedient unto death, even the death of the cross."* And all is crowned by His glorious exaltation: *"God hath highly exalted him."* Christ as God, Christ becoming man, Christ as man in humiliation working out our redemption, and Christ in glory as Lord of all: such are the treasures of wisdom this passage contains.

Volumes have been written on the words this passage contains. And yet insufficient attention has been given to the context in which the Holy Spirit gives this wondrous teaching. It is not a statement of truth for the refutation of error, or the strengthening of faith. The object is a very different one. It was primarily to deal with any pride and lack of love—the setting of Christ's example before them so they would humble themselves as He did. "In lowliness of mind each counting other better than himself. Have this mind in you which was also in Christ Jesus." He who does not study this portion of God's Word with the desire to become humble as Christ was has never used it for the one great purpose for which God gave it. Christ's descent from the throne of God and the humiliation of the cross reveals the only way by which we can ever reach that throne. The faith which, with His atonement, accepts His example too, is alone true faith. Each soul that would truly belong to Him must in union with Him have His Spirit, His disposition, and His image.

"Let this mind be in you, which was also in Christ Jesus, who being in the form of God made himself of no reputation . . . and as a man humbled himself." We must be like Christ in His self-emptying and self-humiliation. In this first great act He emptied himself of His divine glory and power and laid it aside; this was followed up by the no less wondrous humbling of himself as man to the death of the cross. In this amazing twofold humiliation, the astonishment of the universe and the delight of the Father, Holy Scripture with the utmost simplicity tells us how we must be like Christ.

And does God really expect this of us? Why not? or rather, how can He expect anything else? He fully knows the power of human pride. But He also knows that Christ has redeemed us from the power of sin, and that He gives us His resurrection life and power to enable us to live as He did on earth. It is as our example that we not only live through Him but like Him. And further, as our head, He lives in us, and continues in us the life He once led on earth. With such a Christ, and such a plan of redemption, can it be otherwise? The follower of Christ must have the same mind as was in Christ; he must be like Him especially in His humility.

Christ's example teaches us that it is not sin that must humble us. This is what many believers think. They consider sin as necessary to keep us humble. This is not so. There is a true humility that is the beginning of something more, consisting in the acknowledgment of transgression and shortcomings. But there is a humility which is more heavenly still, even like Christ, which consists in the self-abasement that can only wonder that God should bless us, and delights to be as nothing before Him to whom we owe all. It is grace we need, and not sin, to make and keep us humble. The heaviest laden branches always bow the lowest. The greatest flow of water makes the deepest riverbed. The nearer the soul comes to God, the more His majestic presence makes it feel its littleness. It is this alone that makes it possible for each to count others better than himself. Jesus Christ, the holy One of God, is our example of humility: it was knowing that the Father had given all things into His hands, and that He was come from God and went to God, that He washed the disciples' feet. It is the divine presence, the consciousness of the divine life and the divine love in us, that will make us humble.

It appears to many an impossibility to say: "I will not think self. I will esteem others better than myself." They ask grace to overcome the worst outbreaks of pride and vainglory, but an entire self-renunciation, such as Christ's, is too difficult and too high for them. If they only understood the deep truth: "He who humbles himself shall be exalted," "he who loses his life shall find it," they would not be satisfied with anything less than entire conformity to their Lord. And they would find that there is a way to overcome self and self-exaltation: to see it nailed to Christ's cross, and there keep it crucified continually through the Spirit (Gal. 5:24; Rom. 8:13). Only he who heartily yields himself to live in the fellowship of Christ's death can grow to such humility.

To attain this, two things are necessary. The first is a fixed purpose and surrender to be nothing and seek nothing for oneself, to live only for God and our neighbor. The other is faith to appropriate the power of Christ's death as our death to sin and our deliverance from its power. This fellowship of Christ's death brings an end to the life where sin is *too strong for us*; it is the commencement of a life in us where *Christ is too strong for sin*.

It is only under the teaching and powerful working of the Holy Spirit that one can understand and receive this truth. But God be thanked, we have the Holy Spirit. Oh, that we may trust ourselves fully to His guidance! He *will* guide us, it is His work; He *will* glorify Christ in us. He *will* teach us to understand that we are dead to sin and the old self, that Christ's life and humility are ours.

Thus Christ's humility is appropriated by faith. This may take place at once. But the appropriation in experience is gradual. Our thoughts and feelings, our very manners and conversation, have been so long under the dominion of the old self that it takes time to permeate and transfigure them with the heavenly light of Christ's humility. At first the conscience is not perfectly enlightened, the spiritual power of discernment has not yet been exercised. But with each believing renewal of the consecration in the depth of the soul, "I have surrendered myself to be humble like Jesus," power will go out from Him to fill the whole personality—until in face, and voice, and action the sanctification of the Spirit will be observable, and the believer will truly be clothed with humility.

The blessedness of a Christlike humility is unspeakable. It is of great worth in the sight of God: "He giveth grace to the humble." In the spiritual life it is the source of rest and joy. To the humble all that God does is right and good. Humility is always ready to praise God for the least of His mercies. Humility does not find it difficult to trust. It submits unconditionally to all that God says. The two whom Jesus praised for their great faith were those who thought the least of themselves. The centurion had said, "I am not worthy that thou shouldest come under my roof"; the Syrophoenician woman was content to be numbered with the dogs. The humble man does not take offense and is very careful not to give it. He is ever ready to serve his neighbor, because he has learned from Jesus the divine beauty of being a servant. He finds favor with God and man.

Oh, what a glorious calling for the followers of Christ! To be sent into the world by God to prove that there is nothing more divine than self-humiliation. The humble glorifies God, he leads others to glorify Him, he will at last be glorified with Him. Who would not be humble like Jesus?

You who descended from heaven and humbled yourself to the death of the cross have called me to take your humility as the law of my life.

Lord, teach me to understand the absolute need of this. A proud follower of the humble Jesus; this I cannot be. In the secrecy of my heart, in my house, in presence of friends or enemies, in prosperity or adversity, I would be filled with your humility.

My beloved Lord, I sense the need of a new, a deeper insight into your crucifixion and my part in it. Reveal to me how my old proud self is crucified with you. Show me in the light of your Spirit how I am dead to sin and its power, and how in communion with you sin is powerless. Lord Jesus, strengthen in me the faith that you are my life, and that you will fill me with your humility if I will submit to be filled with your Holy Spirit.

Lord, my hope is in you alone. In faith I go into the world to show how the same mind that was in you is also in your children, and teaches us in lowliness of mind each to esteem others better than himself. May God help us. Amen.

22

In the Likeness of His Death

"For if we have been planted together in the likeness of his death, we shall be also in the likeness of his resurrection. For in that he died, he died unto sin once. Likewise reckon ye also yourselves to be dead unto sin, but alive unto God through Jesus Christ our Lord" (Rom. 6:5, 10, 11).

It is to the death of Christ that we owe our salvation. The better we understand the meaning of that death, the richer will be our experience of its power. These verses teach us what it is to be one with Christ in the likeness of His death. Let everyone who desires to be like Christ seek to understand what the likeness of His death means.

Christ had a double work to accomplish in His death. The one was to work out righteousness for us; the other, to obtain life for us. When Scripture speaks of the first part of this work, it uses the expression, *Christ died for our sins.* He took sin upon himself and bore its punishment, making an atonement and bringing in a righteousness in which we could stand before God. When Scripture speaks of the second part of this work, it uses the expression, *He died to sin.* Dying *for sin* has reference to the judicial relation between Him and sin: through His death, atonement is made for sin before God. *Dying to sin* has reference to a personal relation: through His death the connection in which He stood to sin was entirely dissolved. During His life, sin had great power to cause Him conflict and suffering. His death made an end of this. Sin had now no more power to tempt or to hurt Him. He was beyond its reach. Death had completely separated Him and sin. Christ died to sin.

Like Christ, the believer too has died to sin; he is one with Him in the likeness of His death. Just as the knowledge that Christ died for sin as our atonement is indispensable to our justification, so the knowledge that Christ, and we with Him in the likeness of His death, are dead to sin is indispensable to our sanctification. Let us endeavor to understand this.

It was as the second Adam that Christ died. With the first Adam we had joined ourselves together in the likeness of *his* death: he died, and we with him, and the power of his death works in us; we have in very deed died in Him as truly as He himself died. We understand this. In this same way we are joined with Christ in the likeness of His death: He died to sin, and we in Him; and now the power of His death works in us. We are indeed dead to sin, as truly as He himself is.

Through sin, we were made partakers in Adam's death; through the new birth, we become partakers in the death of the second Adam. Every believer who receives Christ is a partaker of the power of His death, and is dead to sin. But a believer may still be very ignorant. Most believers are so occupied with Christ's death *for sin* as their justification that they know little of what it means that in Him they are dead *to sin*. When they discover their need of Him as their sanctification, then the desire is awakened to understand this likeness of His death. They find the secret of holiness in it; that as Christ, so they also have died to sin.

Most believers imagine that sin still has power over them and that they must sometimes obey it. But they think this because they do not know that they, like Christ, are dead to sin. If they understood what this means, their language would be: "Christ has died to sin. Sin has nothing more to say to Him. In His life and death sin had power over Him; it was sin that caused Him the sufferings of the cross and the humiliation of the grave. But He is dead to sin: it has lost all claim over Him. He is entirely and forever freed from its power. Even so am I.

The new life that is in me is the life of Christ from the dead, a life that has been begotten through death, *a life that is entirely dead to sin.*" The believer can glory and say, "Like Christ I am dead to sin. Sin has no right or power over me. I am freed from it; therefore I need not sin."

And if the believer still sins, it is because he does not use his privilege to live as one who is dead to sin. Through ignorance or unwatchfulness or unbelief, he forgets the meaning and the power of this likeness of Christ's death, and sins. But if he maintains his participation with Christ's death, he has the power to overcome sin. He agrees that it is not said, "Sin is dead." No, sin is not dead; sin is very active all around him. But he himself is dead to sin but alive to God; and so sin cannot for a single moment, without his consent, have dominion over him. If he sins, it is because he allows it to reign and submits to it.

You who seek to be like Christ, take the likeness of His death as one of the most glorious parts of the life you covet. Appropriate this first of all in faith. Reckon that you are indeed dead to sin. Let it be settled; God says it is true and you must say it before Him: "Like Christ I am dead to sin." Fear not to say it; it is the truth. Ask the Holy Spirit to enlighten you with regard to this part of your union with Christ, so that it may not only be a doctrine, but power and truth.

Endeavor to understand more deeply what it means to live as dead to sin. In dying you have been freed from its dominion and can now reign in life through Jesus Christ over it. There will follow upon the acceptance of the likeness of His death the conformity of His death (Phil. 3), something that is gradually and increasingly appropriated, as Christ's death manifests its full power in all the faculties and power of your life.

And in order to have the full benefit of this likeness of Christ's death, notice particularly two things. The one is the obligation under which it brings you, "How shall we who are dead to sin live any longer therein?" Endeavor to understand the depths of the meaning of Christ's death into which you have been baptized. His death meant: Rather die than sin: willing to die in order to overcome sin: dead, and therefore released from the power of sin. Let this also be your position: "Know ye not, that as many of us as were baptized into Jesus Christ were baptized into his death?" Let the Holy Spirit baptize you continually deeper into His death until the power of the conformity to Christ's death is discernible in all your walk and conversation.

The other lesson is this: The likeness of Christ's death is not only an obligation but a power. If there is one thing you need more than and above all else, it is this: to know the exceeding greatness of God's power that works in you. It was in the power of God that Christ in His death wrestled with the powers of hell and conquered. You have part with Christ in His death; you have part in all the powers by which He conquered. Yield yourself joyfully and believingly to be led more deeply into the conformity to Christ's death; then you cannot but become like Him.

O my Lord! how little I have understood your grace. I have often read the words, "planted into the likeness of his death," and seen that as you did die to sin, so it is said to believers, "Likewise also ye." But I have not understood its power. And so I have remained bound by the power of sin and as a conqueror who could have had dominion over it. Lord, you have opened to me a glorious prospect. The man who believingly accepts the likeness of your death, and according to your Word reckons himself dead to sin—sin shall not have dominion over him; he has power to live for God.

Lord, let your Holy Spirit reveal this to me more perfectly. I desire to take your Word in simple faith, to take the position you assign me as one who in you is dead to sin. Lord, *in you* I am dead to sin. Teach me to hold fast, or rather to hold you fast in faith, until my whole life is a proof of it. Take me up and keep me in communion with yourself, that, abiding in you, I may find *in you* the death unto sin and the life unto God. Amen.

23

In the Likeness of His Resurrection

"For if we have been planted together in the likeness of his death, we shall be also in the likeness of his resurrection . . . that like as Christ was raised up from the dead by the glory of the Father, even so we also should walk in newness of life" (Rom. 6:5, 4).

Following the likeness of His death is the likeness of His resurrection. To speak only of the likeness of His death, of bearing the cross, and of self-denial gives a one-sided view of following Christ. It is only the power of His resurrection that gives us strength to go on to that conformity to His death which comes as the growth of the inner life. Being dead with Christ refers to the death of the old life to sin and the world; risen with Christ refers to the new life through which the Holy Spirit expels the old. To those who earnestly desire to walk as Christ did, the knowledge of this likeness of His resurrection is indispensable.

We have already seen how the disciples' life before Christ's death was a life of weakness. Sin had power over the disciples, so that Christ could not give them the Holy Spirit, or do for them what He desired. But with the resurrection all was changed. Raised by the almighty power of God, His resurrection life was full of the power of the Spirit. He had conquered sin and death not only for himself but for His disciples, so that He could from the first day make them partakers of His Spirit, of His joy, and of His heavenly power.

When the Lord Jesus makes us partakers of His life, it is not the life that He had before His death but the resurrection life that He won through death. A life in which sin is already ended and put away, a life that has already conquered hell and the devil, the world and the flesh. This is the life that likeness to His resurrection gives us: "In that he liveth, he liveth unto God. Likewise reckon ye also yourselves alive unto God through Jesus Christ our Lord" (Rom. 6:10, 11). Oh, that the Holy Spirit might reveal to us the glory of the life in the likeness of Christ's resurrection! In it we find the power for a life of conformity to Him.

To most believers this is a mystery, and therefore their life is full of sin and weakness and defeat. They believe in Christ's resurrection as the sufficient proof of their justification. They think that He rose simply to continue His work in heaven as mediator. But that He rose that His resurrection life might now be *the very power of their daily life,* they have no idea. They despair upon hearing of following Jesus fully and being conformed to His image. They cannot imagine how it can be required that they should always live like Christ. They do not know Christ in the power of His resurrection, or the mighty power with which His life now works in those who are willing to count all things but loss for His sake (Phil. 3:8; Eph. 1:19, 20). For all who are weary of a life unlike Jesus and who desire to walk in His footsteps, there is in the Scriptures a better life than has been known. The unspeakable treasure of likeness to Christ in His resurrection is yours. Let me ask three questions.

The first is: Are you ready to surrender your life to the rule of Jesus and His resurrection life? No doubt the contemplation of Christ's example has convinced you of sin in more than one point. In seeking your own will and glory instead of God's, in ambition and pride and selfishness and lack of love toward man, you have seen how far you are from the obedience and humility and love of Jesus. The question is whether you will say: "If Jesus will take possesson of my life, then I resign all rights or desire to have or to do my own will. I give Him my entire life with all I have to always do what He through His Word and Spirit shows me. If He will *live and rule in me,* I promise unbounded and hearty obedience."

For such a surrender faith is needed; therefore the second question is: Are you prepared to believe that Jesus will take possession of the life committed to Him, and that He will rule and keep it? When the believer commits his entire spiritual and temporal life to Christ, then he learns to understand Paul's words: "I am dead; I live no more: Christ liveth in me." Dead with Christ and risen again, the living Christ in His resurrection life takes possession of and rules my new life. The resurrection life is not for me to maintain. But blessed be God! *Jesus Christ himself is the resurrection and the life. He himself will daily and hourly see to it and insure that I live as one who is risen with Him.* He does it through that Holy Spirit who is the Spirit of His risen life. The Holy Spirit is in us and will, if we trust Jesus for it, maintain within us the presence and power of the risen Lord. We need not fear that we never can succeed in leading such a holy life. *We are indeed not able.* But it is not required of us. The living Jesus, who is the resurrection, has shown His power over all our enemies. He who so loves us will work it in us. He gives the Holy Spirit as our power, and He will perform His work in us with divine faithfulness if we will only trust Him. *Christ himself is our life.*

And now comes the third question: Are you ready to use this resurrection life for the same purpose that God gave it to Christ, as a power of blessing to the lost? If we are only seeking our own perfection and happiness, it will fail. God raised up and exalted Jesus to give repentance and remission of sins. He ever lives to pray for sinners. Yield yourself to receive His resurrection life with the same aim. Give yourself wholly to working and praying for the perishing; then you will become an instrument in which the resurrection life can dwell and work out its glorious purposes.

Your calling is to live like Christ. To this end *you have been made one with Him* in the likeness of His resurrection. Are you willing to surrender your whole life that He may manifest that resurrection power in every part of it? I pray you do not draw back. Offer yourself unreservedly to Him, with all your weakness and unfaithfulness. Believe that as His resurrection was a wonder above all thought and expectation, so He as the risen One will work in you exceeding abundantly above all you could think or desire.

What a difference there was in the life of the disciples before Jesus' death and after His resurrection! Then all was weakness and fear, self and sin: with the resurrection all was power and joy, life and love, and glory. Just as great a change will come when a believer discovers how the risen One will himself be his life and take on himself the responsibility for the whole of that life. If you are troubled and weary because of a lack of power to walk like Christ, come and taste the blessedness of giving your whole life to the risen Savior in the assurance that He will live it in you.

O Lord, my soul adores you as the prince of life! On the cross you conquered each of my enemies: the devil, the flesh, the world, and sin. As conqueror, you rose to manifest and maintain the power of your risen life in your people. You made them one with yourself in the likeness of your resurrection, now you will live in them, and show forth in their earthly life the power of your heavenly life.

Praise to your name for this wonderful grace. Blessed Lord, I come at your invitation to offer and surrender my life, with all it implies. I have striven in my own strength to live like you, and not succeeded. The more I sought to walk like you, the deeper was my disappointment. I have heard of how blessed it is to cast all care and responsibility for my life on you. Lord, I am risen with you, one with you in the likeness of your resurrection. Come and take me entirely and be my life.

Above all, O my risen Lord, reveal yourself to me as you did to your first disciples in the power of your resurrection. It was not enough that after your resurrection you appeared to your disciples; they did not know you until *you made yourself known to them*. Lord Jesus, I believe in you; *be pleased to make yourself known to me as my life*. It is your work; you alone can do it. I trust you for it. And so my resurrection life shall be a continual source of light and blessing to all who are needing you. Amen.

24

Being Made Conformable to His Death

"That I may know him, and the power of his resurrection, and the fellowship of his sufferings, being made conformable unto his death" (Phil. 3:10).

We know that the death of Christ was the death of the cross. We know that the death of the cross is His chief glory. The one mark by which He is separated from all other persons, both in the divine Being and in God's universe, is this one: He is the crucified Son of God. Of all the articles of conformity, this must necessarily be the chief and most glorious one—conformity to His death.

This is what made it so attractive to Paul. Christ's glory and blessedness must become his glory too: he knows that the most intimate likeness to Christ is conformity to His death. What that death had been to Christ it would be to him, as he was conformed to it.

Christ's death on the cross had been the end of sin. During His life it could tempt Him: when He died on the cross, He died to sin; it could no more reach Him. Conformity to Christ's death is the power to keep us from the power of sin. By the grace of the Holy Spirit I am kept in my position as crucified with Christ, and live out my crucifixion life as the crucified One lives it in me. I am kept from sinning.

Christ's death on the cross was infinitely pleasing to the

Father. If I want to dwell in the favor and love of the Father, I am sure there is nothing that gives such deep and perfect access to it as being conformed to Christ's death. There is nothing in the universe to the Father so beautiful, so holy, so wonderful, as the crucified Jesus. The closer I am to Him the more conformed to His death I can become, and the more I enter into the very bosom of His love.

Christ's death on the cross was the entrance to the power of the resurrection life, the unchanging life of eternity. In our spiritual life we often have to mourn the failures and sins that prove there is still something that prevents the resurrection life from asserting its full power. The secret is: there is still some subtle self-life that has not yet been brought into the perfect conformity of Christ's death. We can be sure that nothing is needed by a fuller entrance into the fellowship of the cross to make us to be full partakers of the resurrection joy.

Above all, it was Christ's death on the cross that made Him the life of the world, gave Him the power to bless and to save (John 12:24, 25). In the conformity to Christ's death there is an end of self: we give ourselves to live and die for others: we are full of the faith that our surrender of ourselves is accepted by the Father. Out of this death we rise, with the power to love and to bless.

But, what is this conformity to the death of the cross? We see it in Jesus. The cross means the death of self—the utter surrender of our own will and our life to be lost in the will of God, to let God's will do with us what it pleases. This was what the cross meant to Jesus. It cost Him a terrible struggle before He could give himself to it. When He was sore amazed and very heavy, and His soul exceedingly sorrowful unto death, it was because His whole being shrank back from that cross and its curse. Three times He had prayed before He could fully say, "Not my will, but thine be done." But He did say it. And His giving himself up to the cross is to say: Let me do anything rather than that God's will should not be done. I give up everything—only God's will must be done.

And this is being made conformable to Christ's death: we so yield our lives to God that we learn to be and to work nothing but what God reveals to us as His will. Such a life is called conformity to the death of Christ because it is himself by His Holy Spirit living in us the life that animated Him in His crucifixion. Were it not for this, the very thought of such conformity would be unthinkable.

In the power of the Holy Spirit, the believer knows that the resurrection life has its power and its glory from its being a crucifixion life, begotten from the cross. He yields himself to it, he believes that it has possession of him. Realizing his failures of the past and that the flesh will assert itself if he allows it to, he yields every power of his being to the place of crucifixion and condemnation. In doing so he is yielding every power of his being, every faculty of body, soul, and spirit to the disposal of Jesus. The distrust and denial of self in everything, the trust of Jesus in everything, mark his life. The very spirit of the cross breathes through his personality.

It is surely not a matter of painful strain and effort to maintain the crucifixion position. It is rest and strength and victory. It is not the dead cross, not self's self-denial, not a work in his own strength that he works with, but the living Jesus, in whom the crucifixion is already passed into the life of resurrection. "I have been crucified with Christ: Christ liveth in me"; this gives the courage and the desire for an ever-growing, ever-deeper entrance into conformity with His death.

And how is this blessed conformity to be attained? Paul gives the answer: "*What things were gain to me*, those I counted loss for Christ. Yea doubtless, and I count *all things* but loss for the excellency of the knowledge of Christ Jesus my Lord . . . that I may know him . . . being made conformable unto his death" (Phil. 3:7–10). The pearl is of great price; but oh! it is worth the purchase. Let us give up all, yes, all, to be admitted by Jesus to a place with Him on the cross.

And if it appears hard to give up all and to choose a whole lifetime on the cross, let us listen to Paul as he tells us what made him so willing. It was Jesus—Christ Jesus, his Lord. The cross was the place where he found the fullest union with his Lord. To know *Him*, to win *Him*, to be found in *Him*, to be made *like to Him*—this was the burning passion that made it easy to cast away all, that gave the cross such mighty attractive power. Anything to come nearer to Jesus. *All for Jesus* was his motto.

It contains the twofold answer to the question, How can one attain this conformity to Christ's death? The one is, cast out all; the other, let Jesus be all.

Yes, it is only knowing Jesus that can make the conformity to His death possible at all. But let the soul win Him, and be found in Him, and know Him in the power of the resurrection, and it becomes more than possible. Therefore, look to Him, the crucified One. Gaze on Him until your soul can say, "Oh, my Lord, I must be like you." Gaze until you see how He, the crucified One, in His ever-present power draws close to live and breathe through your being His crucifixion life. It was through the eternal Spirit that He offered himself to God; that Spirit brings and imparts all that the death on the cross is and effected in you as your life. By the Holy Spirit Jesus maintains in each trusting soul the power of the cross as an abiding death to sin and self, and a never-ceasing source of resurrection life and power. Therefore, look to Him, the living crucified Jesus.

But remember, above all, that while you seek the best and the highest with all your might, the full blessing comes not as the fruit of your efforts, but as a free gift from above. It is as the Lord Jesus reveals himself that we are made conformable to His death. Therefore, seek and get it from Him.

Lord, such knowledge is to wonderful for me. It is high, I cannot attain it. To know you in the power of your resurrection, and to be made conformable to your death—these are things hidden from the wise and prudent and revealed to babes.

O my Lord, I see what utter folly it is to think of likeness to you as an attainment through my effort! I cast myself on your mercy: look upon me according to the greatness of your loving-kindness; and of your free favor reveal yourself to me. Lord, if I will live and die for you, and the souls you have died to save, then you will draw near to me and take me up into the full fellowship of your life and death.

Blessed Savior! I know you are willing. Your love toward us is infinite. Draw me to yourself and take eternal possession of me. And let some measure of conformity to your death, in its self-sacrifice for the perishing, be the mark of my life. Amen.

25

Giving His Life for Men

"Whosoever will be great among you, let him be your minister; and whosoever will be chief among you, let him be your servant; even as the Son of man came not to be ministered unto, but to minister, and to give his life a ransom for many" (Matt. 20:26, 27, 28).

"Hereby perceive we the love of God, because he laid down his life for us: and we ought to lay down our lives for the brethren" (1 John 3:16).

In speaking of being like Christ there is one danger to which even the sincere believer is exposed—seeking it for his own sake, or, as he thinks, for the glory of God in his own personal perfection. The error is common and destructive. It leaves out that which is the essential element in the death of Jesus and in the self-sacrifice it produces: absolute unselfishness in its reference to others. To be made conformable to Christ's death implies a dying to self, a giving up and laying down our life for others. We are to go for others as far as Jesus went, even to laying down our life. We are to consider this the one reason for which we are redeemed and left in the world. Like Christ, the only thing that keeps us in this world is to be the glory of God in the salvation of sinners. Scripture does not hesitate to say that it is in His path of suffering, as He goes to work out atonement and redemption, that we are to follow Him (Matt. 20:28;

Eph. 5:2, 25, 26; Phil. 2:5–8; 1 Pet. 2:21–23).

How clearly this comes out in the words of the Master: "Whosoever will be chief among you, let him be your servant; even as the Son of man came not to be ministered unto, but to minister, and to give his life a ransom for many." The highest in glory will be he who was lowest in service, and joined to the Master in His giving His life a ransom. And, after having spoken of His own death in the words, "The hour is come, that the Son of man should be glorified. Verily, verily, I say unto you, Except a corn of wheat fall into the ground and die, it abideth alone: but if it die, it bringeth forth much fruit," He at once applied this to His disciples: "He that loveth his life shall lose it; and he that hateth his life in this world shall keep it unto life eternal" (John 12:23–25). The corn of wheat dying to rise again, losing its life to regain it multiplied, is clearly set forth as the emblem not only of the Master but of each one of His followers. Loving life, refusing to die, means remaining alone in selfishness: losing life to bring forth much fruit in others is the only way to keep it for ourselves. The only way to find our life is as Jesus did, in giving it up for the salvation of others. Herein is the Father glorified. The deepest underlying thought of conformity to Christ's death is giving our life to God for saving others. Without this, the longing for conformity to that death is in danger of being a refined selfishness.

How remarkably the Apostle Paul exhibited this spirit. He says: "Always bearing about . . . the dying of the Lord Jesus, that the life also of Jesus might be made manifest in our body. For we which live are always delivered unto death for Jesus' sake, that the life also of Jesus might be made manifest in our mortal flesh. So then *death worketh in us, but life in you.*" "Though *he was crucified through weakness, yet he liveth* by the power of God. For *we also are weak in him,* but we shall *live with him by the power of God toward you*" (2 Cor. 4:10–12; 13:4). "Who now rejoice *in my sufferings for you,* and fill up that which is behind of the afflictions of Christ in my flesh for his body's sake, which is the church" (Col. 1:24). These passages teach us how the vicarious element of the suffering that Christ bore in His body on the tree, to a certain extent still characterizes the suffering of His body, the Church. Believers who give themselves up to bear the burden of the sins of men before the Lord, who suffer reproach and shame, weariness and pain, in the effort to win souls, are filling up in their flesh that which is lacking of the afflictions of Christ. The power and the fellowship of His suffering and death work in them; the power of Christ's life through them works in those for whom they labor in love. There is no doubt that in the fellowship of His sufferings and the conformity to His death (Phil. 3), Paul had in view not only the inner spiritual, but also the external bodily participations in the suffering of Christ.

And so it must be with each of us in some measure. Self-sacrifice not merely for the sake of our own sanctification but for the salvation of our fellowmen: this brings us into true fellowship with the Christ who gave himself for us.

The practical application is very simple. Let us first of all *see* the truth the Holy Spirit seeks to teach us. As the most essential thing in likeness to Christ is likeness to His death, so the most essential thing in likeness to His death is the giving up our life to win others to God. It is a death in which all thought of saving self is lost in that of saving others. Let us pray for the light of the Holy Spirit until we know that we are in the world just as Christ was: to love and serve, to live and die, "*even as* the Son of man came not to be ministered unto, but to minister, and to give his life a ransom for many." Oh, that His people would know their calling to God *and to their fellowmen*; that, even as Christ, they are only to live to be a blessing to the world!

Then let us *believe* in the grace that is waiting to make our experience of this truth a reality. Let us believe that God receives our yielding our whole life for His glory in the saving of others. Let us believe that conformity to the death of Jesus in this is what the Holy Spirit will work out in us. Let us above all believe in Jesus: it is He himself who will take every surrendered soul into the full fellowship of His death, of His dying in love to bring forth much fruit. Yes, let us believe, and believing seek from above, as the work and the gift of Jesus, likeness to Jesus in this too.

And let us begin to *act* this faith. Let us put it into practice. Looking upon ourselves as given to live and die for God in our fellowmen, let us with new zeal exercise the ministry of love in winning souls. As we wait for Christ to work out His likeness, as we trust the Holy Spirit to give His mind in us more perfectly, let us in faith begin to act as followers of Him who only lived and died to be a blessing to others. Let our love open the way by the kindness, and gentleness, and helpfulness with which it shines out on all whom we meet in daily life. Let us give ourselves to the work of intercession and expect God to use us as one of His instruments in the answering of those prayers. Let us speak and work for Jesus as those who have a mission and a power from on high. Let us make soul-winning our object. Let us band ourselves with the great army of reapers the Lord is sending out into His harvest. And we shall soon find that giving our life to win others for God is the most blessed way of dying to self, of being even as the Son of man was—a servant of the lost.

Christ gave himself to men, but could not really reach them until He gave himself as *a sacrifice to God* for them. The seed corn died, the life was poured out; then the blessing flowed forth in mighty power. I may seek to love and serve men; but I can only really influence and bless them as I yield myself *to God* and give my life into His hands for them. As I lose myself as an offering on the altar, I become in His spirit and power a blessing. My spirit given into His hands, He can use and bless me.

O most blessed God! do you truly ask me to give myself, my very life, even unto death for my fellowmen? If I have heard the words of the Master correctly, you seek nothing less.

O God! will you indeed have me? Will you permit me, like Christ, to live and die for those around me? to lay myself, I say it in deep reverence, beside Him on the altar of death, crucified with Him, and be a living sacrifice to you for men? Lord, I praise you for this most wonderful grace. And now I come, Lord God, and give myself. Oh, for the grace of the Holy Spirit to make the transaction definite and real! Lord, here I am, given to you, to live only for those whom you are seeking to save.

Blessed Jesus, come and breathe your own mind and love within me. Take possession of me, my thoughts to think, my heart to feel, my powers to work, my life to live, as given to God for men. Write it in my heart: it is done, I am given to God, He has taken me. Keep me in His hands expecting and assured that He will use me. Your giving yourself was followed by the life in power, the outbreaking of the blessing in fullness and power. It will be so in your people too. Glory to your name. Amen.

26

In His Meekness

"Behold, thy king cometh, unto thee, meek" (Matt. 21:5).
"Learn of me; for I am meek and lowly in heart: and ye shall find rest unto your souls" (Matt. 11:29).

It is on His way to the cross that we find the first of these two verses written of our Lord Jesus. It is in His sufferings that the meekness of Jesus is especially manifested. Believers must be ready to take their place under the shadow of His cross, there to behold the Lamb slain for sins. Is it not a precious thought that like the suffering Lamb of God you may bear His image and be like Him every day? You can be meek and gentle even as He was.

Meekness is the opposite of all that is hard or bitter. It has reference to the attitude which we manifest toward our inferiors. "With meekness" we are to instruct those who oppose us, teach and bring back the erring (Gal. 6:1; 2 Tim. 2:25). It expresses our attitude toward superiors: we must "receive the word with meekness" (James 1:21); if the wife is to be in subjection to her husband, it must be in a meek and quiet spirit (1 Pet. 3). As a fruit of the Spirit, meekness ought to characterize all our daily relationships with others (Eph. 4:2; Gal. 5:22; Col. 3:12; Titus 3:2). It is mentioned in Scripture along with humility, because that is the inward disposition concerning oneself, out of which meekness toward others springs.

Perhaps none of the lovely virtues which adorn God's Son is seen more seldom in believers than meekness. There are many who visibly love souls, serve for the salvation of others, and are zealous for God's will and yet who continually come short in this. How often, when offense comes unexpectedly, they are carried away by temper and anger, and have to confess that they have lost the perfect rest of soul in God! There is no virtue for which some have prayed more earnestly; they feel they would give anything if they could keep their temper perfectly and exhibit the meekness and gentleness of Christ. Unspeakable grief and disappointment is experienced by those who have long desired it and yet have not discovered it.

Some excuse their lack of meekness as a certain natural temperament they do not possess. To satisfy themselves they find all sorts of excuses. They do not mean it to be this way. Though the tongue or the temper is sharp, there is still love in their hearts: it just seems to refuse to change. And thus the call to entire conformity to the holy gentleness of the Lamb of God is robbed of its power. And the world is strengthened in its belief that Christians are not much different from other people: though they say, they do not show that Christ changes the heart and life after His own image. And the soul suffers itself and causes unspeakable harm in Christ's church, through its unfaithfulness in appropriating this blessing of salvation.

This grace is of great price in the sight of God. In the Old Testament there are many glorious promises for the meek which were by Jesus gathered up into this one, "Blessed are the meek, for they shall inherit the earth" (Ps. 25:9; 76:9; Prov. 3:34). In the New Testament its praise consists in that meekness gives incomparable beauty to the image of our Lord. A meek spirit is of great price in God's sight; it is the choicest ornament of the Beloved Son. The Father could surely offer no higher inducement to His children, to seek it above all things.

For everyone who desires this spirit, Christ's word is full of comfort and encouragement: "Learn of me; for I am meek." And what will it profit us to learn that *He is meek*? Will it not just make the discovery of our lack of it all the more painful? Lord, teach us how *we* may be meek. The answer is again: "Learn of *me; for I am meek*."

We are in danger of seeking meekness as a gift of which we must be conscious before we practice it. This is not the path of faith. "Moses knew not that his face shone"; he had only seen the glory of God. The soul that seeks to be meek must learn that Jesus is meek. We must take time to gaze on His meekness until the heart has received the full impression: He only is meek; with Him alone can meekness be found. When we realize this, we next fix our hearts on the truth: This meek One is Jesus the Savior. All He is, all He has, is for us. His meekness is to be communicated to us. But He does not impart it apart from himself. When He enters and takes possession of heart and life, He brings His meekness with Him. It is with the meekness of Jesus that we can be meek.

We know how little He succeeded in making His disciples meek and lowly while on earth. It was because He had not yet obtained the new life of the Holy Spirit through His resurrection. But now He can do it. He has been exalted to the power of God to reign in our hearts, to conquer every enemy, and continue in us His own holy life. On earth Jesus was our visible example of this meekness.

"Learn of me; for I am meek and lowly in heart." The word sounds in our ears as our Lord's answer to all the sad complaints on the difficulty of restraining temper. If Jesus is your life and strength, why would He not impart to you His own meekness?

Therefore, only believe! Believe that Jesus is able to fill your heart with His own spirit of meekness. Believe that Jesus himself will accomplish in you the work that you have in vain endeavored to do. *"Behold! thy king cometh unto thee, meek."* Welcome Him to dwell in your heart. Expect Him to *reveal himself to you.* Everything depends on this. Learn of Him that He is meek and lowly of heart, and you shall find rest to your soul.

Precious Savior, grant me now, under the over-shadowing of your Holy Spirit, to draw near and to appropriate your heavenly meekness as my life. Lord, you have not demanded meekness from me without making a provision. You not only save from all sin, but give us your heavenly holiness. Lord, I claim your meekness as a part of the salvation that you have given me. I cannot do without it. How can I glorify you if I do not possess it? Lord, I will learn from you that you are meek. Blessed Lord, teach me. And teach me that you are always with me, always in me as my life. Abiding in you, with you abiding in me, I have you to help me and to make me like yourself.

O holy meekness! you did not come to earth only for a short visit, then to disappear again in the heavens. You are seeking a home. I offer you my heart; come and dwell in it.

Blessed Lamb of God, my Savior and helper, I count on you. Make your meekness to dwell in me. Through your indwelling I am conformed to your image. Oh come, and as an act of your free grace even now, as I wait on you, reveal yourself as my King, meek, and coming in to take possession of me.

"Precious, gentle, holy Jesus,
    Blessed Bridegroom of my heart,
In Thy secret inner chamber,
    Thou wilt show me what Thou art. Amen."

27

Abiding in the Love of God

"As the Father hath loved me, so have I loved you; continue in my love. If ye keep my commandments, ye shall abide in my love; even as I have kept my Father's commandments, and abide in his love" (John 15:9, 10).

Our Lord not only said, "Abide in me," but also, "Abide in my love." Of the abiding in Him, the principal part is the dwelling and being rooted in that wonderful love with which He loves us. "Love seeketh not its own"; it always goes out of itself to live and be at one with the beloved; it ever opens itself and stretches its arms wide to receive and hold fast the object of its desire: Christ's love longs to possess us. Abiding in Christ is an intensely personal relationship, the losing of ourselves in the fellowship of an infinite love, finding our life in the experience of being loved by Him.

Jesus tells us that this love in which we are to abide is the same as the Father's love in which He abides. Surely, if anything were needed to make the abiding in His love more wonderful and attractive, this ought to do so. "As the Father hath loved me, so have I loved you: continue in my love." Our life may be Christlike, unspeakably blessed in the consciousness of an infinite love embracing and delighting in us.

We know this was the secret of Christ's wonderful life, and His strength in prospect of death. At His baptism the voice was heard, the divine message which the Spirit brought and unceasingly maintained in living power, "This is *my beloved Son, in whom I am well pleased.*" More than once we read: "The Father loveth the Son" (John 3:35; 5:20). Christ speaks of it as His highest blessedness: "That the world may know that thou hast . . . loved them, as thou hast loved me . . . thou lovedst me before the foundation of the world"; "That the love wherewith thou hast loved me may be in them" (John 17:23, 24, 26). Just as we live in the light of the sun shining around us, so Jesus lived in the light of the glory of the Father's love shining on Him all the day. It was as *the beloved of God* that He was able to do God's will and finish His work. He dwelt in the love of the Father.

And we too are *the beloved of Jesus. Even as* the Father loved Him, He loves us. What we need to do is to take time to worship and to wait until we see the infinite love of God in all its power and glory streaming forth upon us. Seeing the heart of Jesus we know that His love desires complete possession of us and is offering itself to us as our home and resting place. Oh, if we would but take time to let the wondrous thought fill us, "*I am the beloved of the Lord,* Jesus loves me as the Father loved Him," how the faith would grow!

But there is a second point in the comparison. Not only is the love we are to abide in like that in which He abode, but the way to our abiding is the same as His. As the Son, Christ was in the Father's love when He came into the world; but it was only through obedience that He could abide in it. Nor was this an obedience that cost Him nothing; no, it was through obedience that He suffered, in becoming obedient unto death, even the death of the cross. He kept the Father's commandments and *abode in His love.* "Therefore doth my Father love me, *because* I lay down my life. This *commandment* have I received of my Father." "The Father hath not left me alone; *for I do* always those things that please him." And having given us His example and proved that the path of obedience takes us into the presence and love and glory of God, He invites us to follow Him. "If ye keep my commandments, ye shall abide in my love; even as I kept my Father's commandments, and abide in his love."

Christlike obedience is the way to a Christlike enjoyment of love divine. How it secures our boldness of access into God's presence! "Let us love *in deed and in truth; hereby* shall we assure our hearts before him." Beloved, if our heart condemn us not, then have we *confidence towards God*; and whatsoever we ask, we receive of him, *because we keep his commandments*, and do those things that are pleasing in his sight." How it gives us boldness before men and lifts us above their approval or contempt. We move at God's bidding and know that we have but to obey orders! And what boldness He gives us in the face of difficulty or danger—because we are doing God's will and dare leave to Him all responsibility as to failure or success. The heart filled with the thought of entire obedience to God alone rises above the world into the will of God, into the place where God's love rests on him; like Christ, he abides in the love of God.

Let us seek to learn from Christ what it means to have this spirit of obedience ruling our life. It implies the spirit of dependence; the confession that we have neither the right nor the desire to do anything in our own will. It involves teachableness of spirit. Conscious of the blinding influence of tradition, and prejudice, and habit, it takes its law not from men but from God himself. Conscious of how little the most careful study of the Word can reveal God's will in its spiritual power, it seeks to be entirely under the rule of the Holy Spirit. It knows that its views of truth and duty are very partial and deficient, and counts on being led by God himself to deeper insight and higher attainment.

It has marked God's word, "If thou wilt diligently *hearken to the voice* of the Lord thy God, and wilt *do* that which is right in his sight," and understood that it is only when the commands come from the *living voice* of the Lord heard speaking through the Spirit that the obedience will be possible and acceptable. It sees that following the Father's personal directions, and as a service rendered to Him, that obedience has its full value and brings its full blessing. Its great care is to keep eye and ear open to God for every indication of His blessed will. It is not content with doing right for its own sake; it brings everything into personal relation to God himself, doing it as unto the Lord. It wants every hour and every step in life to be a fellowship with God. It desires in the little things to be consciously obeying the Father, because this is the only way to be prepared for higher work. Its one desire is the glory of God in the triumph of His will. Its one means is with all its heart and strength to be working out that will each moment of the day. And its one reward is this, it knows that through the will of God lies the road deeper into the love of God: "If ye keep my commandments, ye shall abide in my love."

Oh, this blessed Christlike obedience, leading to a Christlike abiding in the divine love! To attain it we must study Christ. He emptied himself and humbled himself and *became obedient.* May He empty us and humble us too! He *learned obedience* in the school of God, and being made perfect became the author of eternal salvation to all *that obey Him.* We must yield ourselves to be taught obedience by Him! We need to listen how He did nothing of himself, but only what He saw and heard from the Father; how entire dependence and continual waiting on the Father was the root of implicit obedience, and this the secret of ever-growing knowledge of the Father's deeper secrets (John 5:19, 20). God's love and man's obedience are as the lock and key fitting into each other. It is God's grace that has fitted the key to the lock; it is man who uses the key to unlock the treasures of love.

In the light of Christ's example and words, what new meaning comes to God's words spoken to His people from of old! "In blessing I will bless thee, and in multiplying I will multiply thee, *because thou hast obeyed my voice.*" "If ye will indeed *obey my voice*, ye shall be a peculiar treasure unto me." "The Lord shall *greatly bless* thee, if thou *only carefully hearken* unto the voice of the Lord thy God, to observe to do all these commandments." Love and obedience indeed become the two great factors in the wonderful relationship between God and man. The love of God, giving himself and all He has to man; the obedience of the believer in that love, giving himself and all he has to God.

We have heard a good deal about full surrender and entire consecration, and thousands praise God for all the blessing He has given them through these words. Let us beware lest we seek for a blessed experience to be enjoyed, or a state to be maintained, while the simple doing of God's will is overlooked. Let us take hold and use this word which God loves: obedience. "To obey is better than to sacrifice." Self-sacrifice is nothing without, it is nothing but, obedience. It was the meek and lowly obedience of Christ, as of a servant and a son, that made His sacrifice such a sweet-smelling savor: it is humble, childlike obedience, first hearkening gently to the *Father's voice*, and then doing that which is right *in His sight*, that will bring us the witness that we please Him.

Dear reader, shall this not be our life? so simple, and sublime: obeying Jesus and abiding in His love.

O my God! what shall I say to the wonderful possibilities you have set before me? Your Son has proven to us how it is possible for a man to live with the love of God always surrounding him. This came by obedience to your voice and will. And because He is ours, our head and our life, we know that we can in our measure live and walk as we see Him do: our souls abiding and rejoicing in your divine love, because you receive our obedience for His sake. My God, it is too wonderful that we are called to this Christlike dwelling in love through the Christlike obedience your Spirit works!

Blessed Jesus, how can I praise you for coming and bringing such a life on earth and making me a sharer in it! O my Lord, I can only yield myself afresh to keep your commandments as you kept the Father's. Lord, impart to me the secret of your own obedience: the open ear, the watchful eye, the meek and lowly heart; the childlike giving of all as the beloved Son to the beloved Father. Savior, fill my heart with your love; in the faith and experience of that love I will do it too. Yes, Lord, this shall be my life: keeping your commandments and abiding in your love. Amen.

28

Led by the Spirit

"And Jesus being full of the Holy Ghost returned from Jordan, and was led by the Spirit into the wilderness" (Luke 4:1).
"Be filled with the Spirit" (Eph. 5:18).
"For as many as are led by the Spirit of God, they are the sons of God" (Rom. 8:14).

From His birth the Lord Jesus had the Spirit dwelling in Him. But there were times when He needed special communications of the Spirit from the Father. Thus it was with His baptism. The descent of the Holy Spirit on Him, the baptism of the Spirit, given in the baptism with water, was a real transaction: He was filled with the Spirit. He returned from the Jordan full of the Holy Spirit, and experienced more manifestly than ever the leading of the Spirit. In the wilderness He wrestled and conquered, not in His own divine power, but as a man who was strengthened and led by the Holy Spirit. In this also "he was in all things made *like* unto his brethren."

The other side of the truth also holds true: the brethren are in all things made like unto Him. They are called to live like Him. This is not demanded from them without their having the same power. This power is the Holy Spirit dwelling in us. As Jesus was filled with the Spirit, and then led by the Spirit, so must we also be filled with the Spirit and be led by the Spirit.

More than once it has seemed almost impossible to be like

Him. We have lived so little for it; we feel completely unable to live like this. Let us take courage in the thought: Jesus himself lived in dependence upon the Spirit. It was after He was filled with the Spirit that He was led by that Spirit to the place of conflict and of victory. And this blessing is ours: we may be filled with the Spirit; we may be led by the Spirit. Jesus, who was himself baptized with the Spirit, has ascended into heaven to baptize us into the likeness with himself. He who would live like Jesus must be baptized with the Spirit. What God demands from His children He first gives. He demands entire likeness to Christ because He will give us, as He did Jesus, the fullness of the Spirit. We must be filled with the Spirit.

This is the reason why the teaching of the likeness to Christ has so little prominence in the Church. Men sought it in their own strength, perhaps with the help of some workings of the Holy Spirit. They did not understand that nothing less was needed than being filled with the Spirit. They thought that real conformity to Christ could not be expected because they had mistaken thoughts about being *filled with the Spirit*. It was thought to be the privilege of a few, and not the calling of every believer. "Be ye filled with the Spirit" is a command to every believer. Only when the Church restores the places for the baptism of the Spirit, and Jesus, as the baptizer with the Spirit, only then will likeness to Christ be sought after and attained. People will then understand and acknowledge: to be like Christ we must be led by the same Spirit; to be led by the Spirit as He was we must be filled with the Spirit. Nothing less than the fullness of the Spirit is absolutely necessary to live a Christlike life.

The way to arrive at it is simple. It is Jesus who baptizes with the Spirit: he who comes to Him desiring it will receive it. All that He requires of us is the surrender of faith to receive what He gives.

The surrender of faith. He asks whether we are committed to following His footsteps, and for this to be baptized of the Spirit. Do not let there be any hesitation as to your answer. First, look on all the promises of His love and of His Spirit, in which the blessed privilege is set forth: *even as I, ye also.* Remember it was of this likeness to himself that He said to the Father: "The glory which thou gavest me have I given them." Think how the love of Christ and the desire to please Him, how the glory of God and the needs of the world, plead with us not to despise this heavenly birthright of being Christlike. Acknowledge the sacred right of ownership Christ has in you, His blood-bought ones: and let nothing prevent your answering: "Yes, dear Lord, as far as is humanly possible, I will be like you. I am completely yours; I must, I will, in all things bear your image. It is for this I ask to be filled with the Spirit."

The surrender of faith: only this, but nothing *less* than this He demands. Let us give what He asks. If we yield ourselves, let it be in the quiet trust that He accepts. At once He begins in secret to cause the Spirit to work more mightily in us. Let us believe it although we do not at once experience it. To be filled with the Holy Spirit, we must wait on our Lord in faith. We can depend upon it that His love desires to give us more than we know. Let our surrender be made in this assurance.

And let this surrender of faith be entire. The fundamental law of following Christ is this: "He who loses his life shall find it." The Holy Spirit comes to take away the old life, and to give in its place the life of Christ in you. Renounce the old life of self-working and self-watching, and believe that the Holy Spirit will renew your life. In the work of the Holy Spirit in you there are no breaks or interruptions: you are in the Spirit as your vital air: the Spirit is in you as your life breath: through the Spirit God works in you both to will and to do according to His good pleasure. Have a deep reverence for the work of the Spirit who dwells within you. Believe in God's power, which works in you through the Spirit to conform you to Christ's life and image moment by moment. Be occupied with Jesus and His life, in the full assurance that the Holy Spirit knows in deep quiet to fulfill His office of communicating Jesus to you. Remember that the fullness of the Spirit is yours in Jesus, a real gift which you accept and hold in faith, even when there is little feeling of it. The feelings may be of weakness and fear and much trembling, and yet the speaking, and working, and living may be in demonstration of the Spirit and of power (1 Cor. 2:3, 4). Live in the faith that the fullness of the Spirit is yours. Entrust the care of your spiritual life to the hands of the Holy Spirit. With the loving presence of Jesus in you, the living likeness to Jesus will be seen on you; the Spirit of life in Christ Jesus dwelling within, the likeness of the life of Christ Jesus will shine around.

And if it does not appear that in believing and obeying your desires are fulfilled, remember that it is in the fellowship with the members of Christ's body, and in the full surrender to Christ's service in the world, that the full power of the Spirit is made manifest. It was when Jesus gave himself to enter into full fellowship with men around Him, and like them to be baptized with water, that He was baptized with the Holy Spirit. And it was when He had given himself in His second baptism of suffering, a sacrifice for us, that He received the Holy Spirit to give to us. Seek fellowship with believers who will with you believe for the baptism of the Spirit: the disciples received the Spirit together with one accord in one place. Band yourself with God's children around you to work for souls; the Spirit is the power from on high to equip for that work: the promise will be fulfilled to the believing, willing servants, who want Him not for their enjoyment but for that work. Christ was filled with the Spirit that He might be enabled to work and live and die for us. Give yourself to such a Christlike living and dying for men, and you may depend that a Christlike baptism of the Spirit, a Christlike fullness of the Spirit, will be your portion.

Blessed Lord, how wondrously you have provided for our growing likeness to yourself in giving us your Holy Spirit. You have told us that it is His work to reveal you, to give your indwelling presence. All the life and holiness and strength we see in you is brought over and imparted and made our very own. He takes of yours, and shows it to us, and makes it ours. Blessed Jesus, we do thank you for the gift of the Holy Spirit.

And now, fill us, oh fill us full, with your Holy Spirit! Lord, nothing less is sufficient. We cannot be led like you, we cannot fight and conquer like you, we cannot love and serve like you, we cannot live and die like you, unless we are full of the Holy Spirit. Blessed be your name! You have commanded, you have promised it; it may, it can, it shall be.

Holy Savior, draw believers together to wait and plead for this. Let their eyes be opened to see the wondrous unfulfilled promises of floods of the Holy Spirit. Let their hearts be drawn to give themselves to live and die for men. And we know it will be your delight to fulfill your office, as He that baptizes with the Holy Spirit and with fire. Glory be to your name. Amen.

29

In His Life Through the Father

"As . . . I live by the Father: so he that eateth me, even he shall live by me" (John 6:57).

Every contemplation of a walk in the footsteps of Christ reveals the need of fixing our attention on the deep living union between the forerunner and His followers. *Like Christ*: the longer we meditate on it, the more we realize how impossible it is without that other: *In Christ*. The outward likeness can only be the manifestation of a living inward union. To do the same works as Christ, I must have the same life. The more I take Him for my example, the more I am driven to Him as my head. Only an inner life essentially like His can lead to a visible walk like His.

What an assuring word we have here: "As I live by the Father; so he that eateth me, even he shall live by me." If you desire to understand your life in Christ, what He will be for you and how He will work in you, you have only to contemplate what the Father was for Him and how He worked in Him. Christ's life in and through the Father is the image of what your life in and through the Son may be.

As Christ's life was a life *hidden in God in heaven*, so must ours be. When He emptied himself of His divine glory, He laid aside the free use of His divine attributes. He came as a man to live by faith; He needed to wait on the Father for wisdom

147

and power as it pleased the Father to impart to Him. He was entirely dependent on the Father; His life was hid in God. Not in virtue of His own independent Godhead, but through the operations of the Holy Spirit, He spoke and acted as the Father.

In the same manner, your life must be hid with Christ in God. Let this encourage you. Christ calls you to a life of faith and dependence, because it is the life He himself led. He has proven its blessedness; He is willing to live His life in you, to teach you also to live in no other way. He knew that the Father was His life, that He lived through the Father, and that the Father supplied His need moment by moment. He assures you that as He lived through the Father, even so you shall live through Him. Take this assurance in faith. Let your heart be filled with the thought of the fullness of life prepared for you in Christ and the abundant supply for all you need. Do not worry over your spiritual life as something you must maintain. Rejoice that you live in the strength of the Lord Jesus, even as He lived through His Father.

As Christ's life was *a life of divine power*, although a life of dependence, so ours *will also be*. He never repented having laid aside His glory to live before God as a man upon earth. The Father never disappointed His confidence; He gave Him all He needed to accomplish His work. Christ experienced the full blessing of living as a man in entire dependence upon His Father, receiving everything day by day from His hands.

Believer, your life can be the same. The divine power of the Lord Jesus will work in and through us. Do not think that your earthly circumstances make a holy life impossible. Jesus manifested the divine life in the midst of earthly surroundings which were supremely difficult. As He lived through the Father, so may you live through Him. Only cultivate greater expectations of what the Lord will do for you. Let it be your sole desire to attain to an entire union with Him. *It is impossible to say what the Lord Jesus would do for a soul who is truly willing to live as entirely through Him as He through the Father.* As the Father worked so gloriously in Christ, so has He undertaken to work all in you.

As the life of Christ was *the manifestation of His union with the Father, so ours also.* Christ says, "Even as the Father has sent me, and I live by the Father." When the Father desired to manifest himself on earth in His love, He could entrust that work to only His beloved Son, who was one with Him. It was because He was the *Son* that the Father sent Him: it was because the Father had sent Him that He must care for the Son's life. In this union rested the certainty that Jesus would live on earth through the Father.

"Even so," Christ said, "he that eateth me, liveth by me." He had said before, "He that eateth my flesh and drinketh my blood dwelleth in me, and I in him." In death He had given His flesh and blood for the life of the world; through faith the soul partakes of the power of His death and resurrection, and receives its right to His life. In the words "whosoever eateth me" is expressed the intimate union and unbroken communion with the Lord Jesus, which is the power of a life in Him. The one great work for the soul, who desires to live entirely by Christ, is to eat Him, daily to feed on Him, to make Him his own.

To attain this, seek continually to have your heart filled with a believing assurance that all Christ's fullness of life is truly yours. Rejoice in the contemplation of His humanity in heaven, and the wonderful provision God has made through the Holy Spirit for the communication of this life to flow unbroken and unhindered down upon you. Thank God unceasingly for the redemption in which He opened the way to the life of God, and for the wonderful life now provided for you in the Son. Offer yourself unreservedly to Him with an open heart and consecrated life that seeks His service alone. In such trust and consecration of faith, with His words abiding in you, let Jesus be your daily food. He who eateth me shall live by me: even as the Father has sent me, and I live by the Father.

Does likeness to Christ begin to seem possible in the light of this promise? He who lives through Christ can also live like Him. Therefore let the wonderful life of Christ on earth be the object of your adoring contemplation until your whole heart understands and accepts the word, *"Even so, he who eateth me shall live through me."* The same Christ who set us the example works in us from heaven that life which can live out the example. Our life will become a continual song: To Him who lives in us, in order that we may live like Him, be the love and praise of our hearts. Amen.

O my God, how shall I thank you for this wonderful grace! Your Son became man to teach us the blessedness of a life of dependence on the Father; He lived through the Father. We see in Him how the divine life can live and work and conquer on earth. And now He is ascended into heaven and has all power to let that life work in us. We are called to live even as He did on earth: we live through Him. O God, praise to your name for this unspeakable grace!

Lord, hear the prayer that I now offer to you. Show me more of Christ's life through the Father. I need to understand if I am to live as He did! Oh, give me the spirit of wisdom in the knowledge of *Him*! Then I shall know what I may expect from Him, what I can do through Him. It will no longer be a struggle and an effort to live according to your will. I shall know that His blessed life on earth is mine, according to the word, "Even as I through the Father, so ye through me." Then I will daily feed upon Christ in the joyful experience that I live through Him. O Father, grant this in full measure for His name's sake! Amen.

30

In Glorifying the Father

"Father, the hour is come; glorify thy Son, that thy Son also may glorify thee. I have glorified thee on the earth" (John 17:1, 4).

"Herein is my Father glorified, that ye bear much fruit; so shall ye be my disciples" (John 15:8).

The glory of an object is when its intrinsic worth and excellence answers perfectly to all that is expected of it. That excellence or perfection may be so hidden or unknown that the object has no visible glory to those who behold it. To *glorify* is to remove every hindrance, and to so reveal the full worth and perfection of the object that its glory is seen and acknowledged by all.

The highest perfection of God is His holiness. In it righteousness and love are united. As the holy One He hates and condemns sin. As the holy One He also frees the sinner from its power, and raises Him to communion with himself. His name is "The holy One of Israel, thy Redeemer." The song of redemption is "Great is the holy One of Israel in the midst of thee." To the Blessed Spirit, whose special work it is to maintain the fellowship of God with man, the title of Holy in the New Testament belongs more than to the Father or the Son. It is this holiness, judging sin and saving sinners, which is the glory of God. For this reason the two words are often found together. So in the song of Moses: "Who is like thee, *glorious* in *holiness?*" So in the song of Seraphim: "*Holy, holy, holy,* is the Lord of hosts; the whole earth is full of his *glory.*" And so in the song of the Lamb: "Who shall not *glorify* thy Name? for thou only art *holy.*" As has been well said: "God's glory is His manifested holiness; God's holiness is His hidden glory."

When Jesus came to earth to glorify the Father, He demonstrated in its true light and beauty that glory which sin had so entirely hidden from man. Man had been created in the image of God that God might place His glory upon him—that God might be glorified in him. The Holy Spirit says, "Man is the image and glory of God." Jesus came to restore man to his high destiny: He laid aside the glory which He had with the Father, and came in our weakness and humiliation to teach us how to glorify the Father on earth. God's glory is perfect and infinite: man cannot contribute any new glory to God. He can only reflect the glory of God. God's holiness is His glory. As this holiness of God is seen in man, God is glorified; His glory as God is demonstrated.

Jesus glorified God *by obeying Him.* In giving His commandments to Israel, God continually said, "Be ye holy, for I am holy." In keeping them they would be transformed into a life of harmony with Him and enter into fellowship with Him as the holy One. In His conflict with sin and Satan, in His sacrifice of His own will, in His waiting for the Father's teaching, in His unquestioning obedience to the Word, Christ showed that He counted nothing worth living for except to let this holy God really *be God,* His will alone acknowledged and obeyed. Because He alone is holy, His will alone should be done, and so His glory be shown in us.

Jesus glorified God *by confessing Him.* He not only taught the message God had given Him, but there is something far more striking. He continually spoke of His own personal relationship to the Father. He did not silently trust the influence of His holy life. He wanted men to distinctly understand what the root and aim of that life was. Time after time He told them that He came as a servant sent from the Father, that He totally depended upon Him, that He only sought the Father's honor, and that all His happiness was to please the Father.

Jesus glorified God *by giving himself for the work of His redeeming love*. God's glory is His holiness, and God's holiness is His redeeming love—love that triumphs over sin by conquering the sin and rescuing the sinner. Jesus not only told of the Father being the righteous One, whose condemnation must rest on sin, and the loving One, who saves everyone who turns from his sin, but He gave himself to be a sacrifice to that righteousness, a servant to that love, even unto death. It was not only in acts of obedience or words of confession that He glorified God, but in giving himself to magnify the holiness of God, to vindicate at once His law and His love by His atonement. He gave himself, His whole life and being, to show how the Father loved, how the Father must condemn the sin, and yet would save the sinner. He counted nothing too great a sacrifice. He lived and died only that the glory of the Father, the glory of His holiness, of His redeeming love, might break through the dark veil of sin and flesh, and shine into the hearts of the children of men. As He himself expressed it in the last week of His life, when the approaching anguish began to press in upon Him: "Now is my soul troubled. And what shall I say? Father, save me from this hour: but for this cause came I unto this hour: Father, glorify thy name." And the assurance came that the sacrifice was well-pleasing and accepted, in the answer: "I have both glorified it, and will glorify it again."

Jesus as man was prepared to have part in the glory of God. He sought it in the humiliation on earth; He found it on the throne of heaven. And so He became our forerunner, leading many children to glory. He shows us that the sure way to the glory of God in heaven is to live only for the glory of God on earth. Yes, this is the glory of a life on earth: glorifying God here, we are prepared to be glorified with Him forever.

Is this not a wonderful calling, blessed beyond all conception—calling to live only to glorify God, to let God's glory shine out in every part of our life? Our daily life, down to its most ordinary acts, may be transparent with the glory of God. Oh! let us study this trait of the wondrous image of our Jesus: He glorified the Father. Let us listen to Him as He points us to the high aim, *that your Father in heaven may be glorified*, and as He shows us the way, *"herein is my Father glorified."* Let us remember how He told us that when He answers our prayer, this would still be His object: *"That the Father may be glorified in the Son."* Let our whole life, like Christ's, be so animated by this as its ruling principle that our watchword becomes: *All to the glory of God.* And let our faith hold fast the confidence that in the fullness of the Spirit there is ample provision for our desire being fulfilled: "Know ye not that your body is the temple of the Holy Spirit which is in you? . . . Therefore glorify God in your body and in your spirit" (1 Cor. 6:19, 20).

If we want to know the way, let us again study Jesus. He obeyed the Father. Let simple obedience mark our whole life. Let humble, childlike waiting for direction, a Christlike dependence on the Father's showing us His way, be our daily attitude. Let everything be done to the Lord, according to His will, for His glory, in direct relationship to himself. Let God's glory shine out in the holiness of our life.

He confessed the Father: He did not hesitate to speak of His personal relationship with the Father. It is not enough that we live right before men: how can they understand if there be no interpreter? They need as a personal testimony to hear that what we are and do is *because we love the Father and are living for Him.* The witness of the life and the words must go together.

And He gave himself to the Father's work. So He glorified Him. He showed sinners that God has a right to have us wholly for himself, that God's glory alone is worth living and dying for, and that as we give ourselves to this, God will most wonderfully use and bless us. It was that men might glorify the Father in heaven that Jesus lived, and that we must live too. Oh, let us give ourselves to God for men; let us plead, and work, and live, and die that men may see that God is glorious in holiness, that the whole earth may be filled with His glory!

Believer, "the Spirit of God and of glory, the Spirit of holiness, rests upon you." Jesus delights to do in you His beloved work of glorifying the Father. Fear not to say: Oh, my Father, in your Son, like your Son, I will only live to glorify you.

O my God, show me your glory! I know how utterly impossible it is by my own effort to lift myself up or bind myself to live for your glory alone. But if you will reveal your glory, if you will make all your goodness pass before me, if you will let your glory shine into my heart, I will never be able to do anything but glorify you. I will live to make known what a glorious holy God you are.

Lord Jesus, give me by your Holy Spirit a sight of how you lived. Teach me the meaning of your obedience to the Father, your acknowledgment that, at any cost, His will must be done. Teach me by your confession of the Father and by your personal testimony to tell men what He was to you. Let my lips too tell out what I taste of the love of the Father that men may glorify Him. And above all, teach me that it is in saving sinners that redeeming love has its triumph and its joy, that it is in holiness casting out sin that God has His highest glory. And so take possession of my whole heart that I may love and labor, live and die, for this one thing, "That every tongue should confess that Jesus Christ is Lord, *to the glory of God the Father.*"

O my Father, let the whole earth, let my heart, be filled with your glory! Amen.

31

In His Glory

"We know that, when he shall appear, we shall be like him; for we shall see him as he is. And every man that hath this hope in him purifieth himself, even as he is pure" (1 John 3:2, 3).

"And I appoint unto you a kingdom, as my Father hath appointed unto me" (Luke 22:29).

God's glory is His holiness. To glorify God is to yield ourselves that God in us may show forth His glory. It is only by yielding ourselves to be holy, to let His holiness fill our life, that His glory can shine forth from us. The one work of Christ was to glorify the Father, to reveal what a glorious God He is. Our one work is, like Christ's, by our obedience, and testimony, and life, to make known our God as "glorious in holiness" that He may be glorified in heaven and earth.

When the Lord Jesus had glorified the Father on earth, the Father glorified Him with himself in heaven. This was not only His just reward; it was a necessity in the very nature of things. There is no other place for a life given to the glory of God, as Christ's was, than in that glory. The law holds true for us too: a heart that thirsts for the glory of God, that is ready to live and die for it, becomes prepared to live in it. *Living for God's glory* on earth is the gate to *living in God's glory* in heaven. If with Christ we glorify the Father, the Father will with Christ glorify us too. Yes, we shall be like Him in His glory.

We shall be like Him in *His spiritual glory*, the glory of His holiness. In the union of the two words in the name of the Holy Spirit, we see that what is *holy* and what is *spiritual* stand in the closest connection with each other. When Jesus as man had glorified God by revealing, and honoring, and giving himself to His holiness, He was taken as man into and made a partaker of the divine glory.

And so it will be with us. If here on earth we have given ourselves to have God's glory take possession of us, and God's holiness, God's Holy Spirit, dwells and shines in us, then our human nature with all our faculties shall have poured into and transfused through it the purity and the holiness and the life, the very brightness of the glory of God.

We shall be like Him *in His glorified body*. It has been well said: Embodiment is the end of the ways of God. The creation of man was to be God's masterpiece. In man there was to be a spirit in a physical body lifting up and spiritualizing the body into its own heavenly purity and perfection. Man as a whole is God's image, his body as much as his spirit. In Jesus a human body is set upon the throne of God, is found a worthy partner and container of the divine glory. Our bodies are going to be the objects of the most astonishing miracle of divine transforming power: "He will change our vile body . . . like unto his glorious body, according to the working whereby he is able even to subdue all things unto himself" (Phil. 3:21). The glory of God as seen in our bodies, made like Christ's glorious body, will be something almost more wonderful than in our spirits. We are "waiting for the adoption, to wit, the redemption of our body."

We shall be like Him *in His place of honor*. Every object must have a proper place for its glory to be seen. Christ's place is the central one in the universe: the throne of God. He spoke to His disciples, "Where I am, there shall my servant be. If any man serve me, *him will my Father honor*." "I appoint unto you a kingdom, as my Father hath appointed unto me; that ye may eat and drink at my table, and sit on thrones judging the twelve tribes of Israel." To the church at Thyatira He says: "He that overcometh, and keepeth my works unto the end, to him will I give power over the nations . . . even as I received of my Father."

And to the church at Laodicea: "To him that overcometh will I grant to sit on my throne, even as I overcame, and am set down with my Father on his throne." Higher and closer it cannot be: "Even as we have borne the image of the earthly, we shall also of the heavenly." The likeness will be complete and perfect.

Such divine glimpses into the future reveal to us, more than all our thinking, what intense truth, what divine meaning there is in God's creative word: "Let us make man in our image, after our likeness." To show forth the likeness of the invisible, to be a partaker of the divine nature, to share with God His rule of the universe, is man's destiny. His place is indeed one of unspeakable glory. Standing between two eternities—the eternal purpose in which we were predestinated to be conformed to the image of the firstborn Son, and the eternal realization of that purpose when we shall be like Him in His glory—we hear the voice from every side: Image-bearers of God! Share the glory of God and of Christ! Live a Godlike, live a Christlike life!

"I shall be satisfied when I awake with thy likeness," so the Psalmist sang. Nothing can satisfy the soul but God's image, because that is what it was created for. It is as a partaker of that likeness that we shall be satisfied. Blessed are they who desire it with insatiable hunger; they shall be filled. This, the very likeness of God, will be the glory streaming down on them from God himself, streaming through their whole being, streaming out from them through the universe. "When Christ who is our life shall be manifested, we also shall be manifested with him in glory."

Nothing can be made manifest in that day that has not a real existence here in this life. If the glory of God is not our life here, it cannot be hereafter. It is impossible; he alone who glorifies God here can God glorify hereafter. "Man is the image and glory of God." It is as you bear the image of God here, as you live in the likeness of Jesus, who is the brightness of His glory and the express image of His person, that you will be fitted for the glory to come. If we are to be as the Christ in glory, we must first bear the image of Christ in humiliation.

Child of God, Christ is the uncreated image of God. Man is His created image. On the throne in glory the two will be eternally one. You know what Christ did, how He drew near, how He sacrificed all to restore us to the possession of that image. Shall we not yield ourselves to this wonderful love, to this glory inconceivable, and give our life wholly to manifest the likeness and the glory of Christ? Shall we not, like Him, make the Father's glory our aim and hope, living to His glory here as the way to live in His glory there?

The Father's glory: it is in this that Christ's glory and ours have their common origin. Let *the Father* be to us what He was to Him, and the Father's glory will be ours as it is His. All the traits of the life of Christ converge to this as their center. He was the Son; He lived as the Son; God was to Him *Father.* As the Son He sought the Father's glory; as the Son He found it. Let this be our conformity to the image of the Son, that *the Father* is the all in all of our life; the Father's glory must be our everlasting home.

Beloved brethren, who have accompanied me thus far in these meditations on the Christlike life, the time is now come for us to part. Let us do so with the word, *"We shall be like him; for we shall see him as he is. And every man that hath this hope in him purifieth himself, even as he is pure." Like Christ!* Let us pray that this may be the one aim of our faith, the one desire of our heart, the one joy of our life. Oh, what will it be when we meet in the glory, when we see Him as He is, and see each other all like Him!

Ever blessed and most glorious God, what thanks shall I give for the glorious gospel of Christ, who is the image of God, and for the light of your glory which shines upon me in Him? And what thanks shall I render you, that in Jesus I have seen the image not only of your, but of my glory, the pledge of what I am to be with you through eternity?

O God, forgive me for Jesus' sake that I have so little believed this, that I have so little lived this. And I beseech you to reveal *the glory* in which I am to live eternally, in which I can be living even now. O Father, awaken me to see and feel what your purpose with me is. I am indeed to spend eternity in your glory: your glory is to be around me, and on me, and in me; I am to be like your Son in His glory. Father, I beseech you, oh, visit your Church! Let the Holy Spirit, the Spirit of glory, work mightily in her; and let this be her one desire, the one mark by which she is known: the glory of God resting upon her.

Our Father, grant it for Jesus' sake! Amen.